Declutter Your Data

Take Charge of Your Data and Organize Your Digital Life

Angela Crocker

Self-Counsel Press acknowledges the financial support of the Government of Canada for our publishing activities. Canadä

Printed in Canada.

First edition: 2018

Library and Archives Canada Cataloguing in Publication

Crocker, Angela, author

Declutter your data : take charge of your data and organize your digital life / Angela Crocker. — First edition.

(Reference series)
Issued in print and electronic formats.
ISBN 978-1-77040-297-3 (softcover).—ISBN 978-1-77040-484-7 (EPUB).—ISBN 978-1-77040-485-4 (Kindle)

1. Time management. 2. Personal information management.
I. Title. II. Series: Self-counsel reference series

HD30.2.C675 2017   650.1'1   C2017-904977-1
                                        C2017-904978-X

Self-Counsel Press
(a division of)
International Self-Counsel Press Ltd.

Bellingham, WA   North Vancouver, BC
       USA   Canada

Contents

Download Kit

Samples

Notice to Readers

Laws are constantly changing. Every effort is made to keep this publication as current as possible. However, the author, the publisher, and the vendor of this book make no representations or warranties regarding the outcome or the use to which the information in this book is put and are not assuming any liability for any claims, losses, or damages arising out of the use of this book. The reader should not rely on the author or the publisher of this book for any professional advice. Please be sure that you have the most recent edition.

Dedication

For Paul, my husband, who keeps our lives running when I disappear in writer mode, and our son, Sean, my loyal cohost, who knows how to look after his tea-loving Mamma.

Acknowledgments

Being a writer can be a lonely undertaking. Thankfully, I have an amazing group of family, friends, and colleagues to help my star shine bright.

Thank you to Brian, my dear ol' Dad, who never wavers as my truest fan, and my brother, Michael, who always checks in.

Thank you to Vicki McLeod and Rebecca Coleman for giving me a safe place to think aloud, and to Karley Cunningham for her laser-focused questions to keep priorities top of mind.

Thank you to Peggy Richardson and Kim Plumley for great soup and all that comes with it.

Thank you to Eileen Velthuis, who makes writing a joy by simultaneously seeing the big picture and the tiny details.

Thank you to Mike Vardy, who continues to teach this productive person new ways to be productive.

Thank you to Paul Holmes, Chris Burdge, Katharine Holmes, Sean Smith, and all my Social Media Camp family for championing my work.

Thank you to my fellow authors and speakers in social media, online communities, digital marketing, and related pursuits. Collectively, your work helps everyone make the most of their digital footprint.

Thank you to my Masters of Education cohort at Simon Fraser University. Together with our professors, we're making the future bright for students of all ages through education technology and learning design.

Thank you to my associates, especially to Heather Fowlie and Kimmy Dean, for all your superhero efforts to help me share my work with the world.

And, finally, thank you to eight-year-old Pippa for reminding me of the sheer joy of seeing my name (and now hers) in print.

Part I
Why Digital Decluttering Matters

Digital decluttering is the process of organizing your data and technology in ways that support your lifestyle. To get started, you need to be clear on what digital clutter is and why decluttering is important to you. In this part, we'll explore the digital clutter problem, the benefits of digital decluttering, and how the process works.

Introduction

Welcome to *Declutter Your Data*. Simply by reading this book you'll be better equipped to take charge of your digital life. Read on and you'll have a plan with concrete action steps to organize your information and declutter your data. You'll also figure out why data decluttering is important to you.

I'm Angela Crocker, your guide to take charge of your data and organize your digital life. I've been living with computers since 1979 and have been on the Internet for more than 25 years. I've watched online technologies evolve and observed how this evolution has changed our lives at home and in the office. The pace of change is extraordinary! The rate at which we've adopted new technologies and improvements to Internet upload and download speeds are impressive. Add to that the evolution from pagers to smartphones and the increased power of the computer for even more change.

However, all that change has created a problem: Digital clutter.

Before we dive in, it may be helpful to pause a moment and consider what digital cluttering means to you. How do you define it? How does digital clutter make you feel? How does it impact your life? What prompted you to pick up this book? Throughout the digital decluttering process, we'll pause to complete short exercises to help you along your digital decluttering journey. See Sample 1: Preconceptions about Digital Decluttering, and then find the worksheet on the digital download kit included with this book, for you to complete.

Sample 1: Preconceptions about Digital Decluttering

Date:
What does digital decluttering mean to you?
Digital clutter is all my unorganized computer files. I have too many documents, emails, photographs, and more. The clutter makes me feel stressed. I'm tired of struggling to find information I know is on my computer. I waste time looking for emails and misplaced files. I keep forgetting my passwords. I bought this book because I need help. I need someone to guide me. What can I do with my mess?

1. The Digital Clutter Problem

Digital clutter is a fairly new problem. Our ancestors may have lived with too many objects but they didn't live with the same volume of information. By ancestors I mean our parents just one generation back. Some grew up with analog information and have had to adapt to digital living while others were born into the digital life. For both groups, digital clutter is an artifact of the Internet, personal computers, social networking, and smart devices. We now consciously create and unconsciously contribute to terabytes of data every year.

Our personal collection of data started slowly. With home and office computers, work previously done by hand or with typewriters and adding machines, moved into word processing and spreadsheet software. Files were stored on floppy disks and rudimentary hard drives. In 1993, there were about 600 websites. Early Internet adopters may have accessed those first websites, a few Bulletin Board System (BBS) message boards and, possibly, had an ICQ identity. I seek you, remember?

Flash forward and today we live with what Terry O'Reilly calls "too much data smog." (*This I Know: Marketing Lessons from Under the Influence)*, Knopf Canada, 2017). We have millions of websites and years' worth of YouTube videos to watch plus social networking and cloud storage. Add to that our mobile phones, tablets, laptops, and smart home devices. We have vast search histories and medical, financial, and shopping digital records. And let's not forget any lingering remnants of data from our older collections of USB drives, SD cards, and defunct computers. Think back to when you first started using a computer. How much data have you created since then? How much information have you accessed? As R "Ray" Wang notes in his book *Disrupting Digital Business* (Harvard Business Review Press, 2015), "The volume of data we capture is already beyond human comprehension."

To quantify that data think in terabytes (TB). You know, bytes, kilobytes, megabytes, gigabytes, terabytes, and so on. *The Register* recently quoted a Western Digital Corporation finding that the "average US household has 41.5 TB of data spread across 14 digital devices, and this is only going to grow" (www.theregister. co.uk/2017/08/31/wdc_home_nas_box/, accessed September, 2017). That 41.5 TB can hold more than 1 million hours of 1080 HD video or nearly 21 million digital photos of 2 MB each or trillions of pages of text. That's just the average per household!

Unfortunately, as Nancy Collier observed in her book *The Power of Off*, (Sounds True, 2016), "We spend a lot of our time just clearing the junk, which we're now forced to do in order to discover anything we might actually care about." By sheer volume alone, I'm certain everyone needs to do some data decluttering.

2. Benefits of Digital Decluttering

No matter its origins, digital information is central to our way of living today. As a result, we've got to take ownership of our digital footprint. Beyond simply clearing the clutter, there are many benefits. Better organization means efficiency and, if time is money, it improves your bottom line. By knowing what information you have and where to find it, you can make the most of your time both online and offline. In doing so, you reduce the amount of information you have to process — what psychologists call "cognitive load" — and self-administer the antidote to information overwhelm.

That recovered time and reduced cognitive load can be used to nurture your interests and try new things. Furthermore, reducing the digital noise around you minimizes distractions and creates space to focus on more complex projects, including analog projects away from your computer.

Digital decluttering also creates space for self-care. Taking control of the amount of time you spend online allows you to focus on what's important to you. Time away from the screen is the best prevention for "sitting disease," a term I first heard from the pelvic health specialist, Kim Vopni. Less screen time can also improve your sleep patterns, protect your hearing, and give your eyes a much needed rest.

That same self-care space allows you to nourish meaningful relationships, reigniting your listening skills and ability to focus. Genuine connections are often lost in the digital clutter and rekindling the skills to foster those connections benefit all. If you're a parent or other role model for children and youth, demonstrating the healthy use of technology is one of the best ways to pass on this digital life lesson.

In addition to the practical, physical, and social benefits of digital decluttering, you may find peace in other aspects of your life. Understanding your data and how you use technology can highlight the myths of the perfectly polished life. What is published online is often a curated collection of posts that perpetuate the myth of the perfect life. Knowing this can reduce envy and your need to "keep up with the Joneses."

Similarly, understanding your data can help you find the elements that are key in your quest for digital happiness. While this book is about organizing data, it is also designed to advocate for informed digital living. I want you to use data and technology to build your ideal life. If you love taking photographs, then take photographs! If Instagram Stories make you happy, then create and view them. However, I want you to put strategies in place to put boundaries around your use of technology so that the digital parts of your life are fulfilling, not draining.

Digital decluttering can also be a good reminder of the privilege of digital access. Not all sectors of society nor all places in the world have such ready access to technology and information. By noting this privilege, we can be appreciative of the opportunity rather than burdened by the requirements of digital living. This awareness can also complement the trend towards minimalism. Just as we limit our material possessions to those most useful and those that spark joy, as decluttering expert Marie Kondo (author of *The Life-Changing Magic of Tidying Up*, Ten Speed Press, 2014) put it, we can also limit our digital possessions. As my Dad often says, let's collect memories, not things.

Digital decluttering also allows you to prepare your digital legacy. Long after you've passed away, your information will still be available. It's not easy to think about our own mortality but it has become an essential part of estate planning. While alive, you get to decide what information you leave behind and who will have access to it after you're gone. If you don't make arrangements in advance, some data may become inaccessible and other data might be used in undesirable ways.

As you can see, time invested in digital decluttering has many benefits. I consider myself an advocate for living an integrated digital life that includes both digital and analog components. An integrated digital life includes the mindful use of technology to achieve your goals. You choose what devices you have and how you use them. And, whenever possible, use the power you have to decide what data you create and what data you keep.

3. What to Do about It?

Whether you like it or not, digital clutter is inevitable. Only the most diligent have taken time to be rigorous about deleting old files, organizing current files, and so on. More often the solution is to buy more storage to house an ever growing data collection. If, like me, you've got some digital clutter to sort, keep reading. Together we'll explore the kinds of data in your life, and strategies, lots of strategies, to help you manage your information. Think of it as a digital cleanse.

Digital clutter is a sneaky thing. Unlike the surplus gadgets in your kitchen, data hides on your computer, your smartphone, and in the cloud. It also festers within your credit card purchase history, schoolwork, medical records, driver's abstract, and any legal proceedings you've been party to. Yet much of this information is largely invisible. Sure, you walk by your computer daily or pick up your smartphone frequently but the information within is in a nice tidy package. Only when you start looking for something specific are you likely to realize that you have too many emails, digital photographs, or other files. The volume and variety of information can be a burden in ways you might not even realize.

After 25 years on the Internet, I can relate. I had an unwieldy amount of data. I was storing 40,000 high-resolution photographs, thousands of work files, and hundreds of presentations. I had dozens of partly written blog posts and about 450 social network accounts, mostly for research purposes. Add to that 700 apps and extensive digital music and movie libraries. Plus, for some unknown reason, I still had a raft of university essays leftover from my undergraduate days at Simon Fraser University. With files stored on multiple hard drives, two mobile devices, several server back-ups and more in the cloud on Dropbox, iCloud, and Google Drive, I had a lot of data to declutter.

Sound familiar? Don't worry. You're not alone. Few individuals, and even fewer businesses, truly know what information they have available nor where to find it. I tackled my digital clutter and learned a lot along the way. Truthfully, it's an ongoing process and I've still got aspects of my data to wrangle.

In this book, I share wisdom, best practices, and strategies to help you reduce the digital clutter in your life. Think of it as a menu you can customize to declutter your data. It's a series of customizable options, not a single curative prescription.

4. Is Digital Decluttering for you?

Is this for you? Yes! Almost everyone today has some degree of excess data. At home, that might just be an overflowing email inbox and a photo archive bursting at the seams. Add to that some social media accounts and I'm sure you have digital clutter. Work situations are also filled with surplus data, adding to the volume of information for which you are responsible.

If you're interested in making better use of technology, sorting through your digital clutter, and coming up with an organized and efficient way to access your data, digital decluttering is definitely for you. Applying the strategies in this book will reduce your digital clutter, make you more efficient, save you time, and give you a happier relationship with your information.

Even if you're a clutter bug, happy to live with endless digital piles of digital possessions, I urge you to read this book. It's OK if you stalwartly refuse to delete any messages in your email inbox. I get it. But you can still pick and choose amongst the strategies in this book. Reducing your data, securing your data, and making plans for your digital legacy are essential for all.

5. How the Process Works

Declutter Your Data is designed to help you understand why you want to organize your information, what kinds of data you have to cope with, and strategies to take charge of your digital footprint. While you can work through this book in any order, I suggest you start by understanding why you want to do this. Then, your decluttering efforts will be driven by a clear purpose. This will motivate you to keep going when the data sorting gets tedious or overwhelms you. By understanding your purpose before moving on to the specific strategies you'll also be better able to pick the strategies that suit your custom blend of digital clutter. If your email inbox is pristine, then skip the chapter on email, for example.

If you've got a wide range of data, as most of us do, I suggest you work through the strategies in the order listed. I've tried to sequence them so you'll have some early success before the tougher, time-consuming tasks make it onto your to-do list. That said, if you can't take action on a particular strategy today, feel free to move on to the next one, just remember to loop back to any skipped strategies. Once completed, your digital life will have moved away from chaos and closer to serene.

Throughout the book, you'll find references to the workbook which contains a variety of worksheets. These are designed to help you understand your reasons, explore your data and facilitate your implementation of the digital decluttering strategies. A digital download of the workbook is included with the purchase of this book, if you need to print a copy (see the end of the book for instructions on accessing it). Complete the forms as they apply to your situation. There is no penalty for skipping one if it's irrelevant to your data. I hope most of them will be helpful to you and encourage you to complete as many as makes sense for you.

6. The Commitment to the Digital Cleanse

For more than three years, I have worked to declutter my data and sort my technology. The ideas in this book come from hands on experience and careful research. I'm delighted to share them with you. If you've got data overload, you need a digital cleanse, too.

There are three main phases to the process. First, you'll explore why data decluttering is important to you. Next comes a larger effort to wrestle with your complete data collection. Likely, you've got years' worth of data to sort through and delete, filter, and organize. This phase may take you many weeks, months, or even years. In my experience, just when you think you've decluttered all your data, you'll find another pocket stashed on a hard drive that needs your attention. At every step, you decide what to keep whether it's merely practical or it brings you joy. In a sense, this is a perpetual process that's never complete especially as you're constantly creating new data. Which brings us to the third phase: maintenance.

Once decluttered, you must have an ongoing commitment to your keep your data organized. Small daily efforts should be all that's required. In the event that your first digital decluttering efforts aren't maintained daily, you may have to declutter again from time to time. Perhaps it's something you add to your annual spring cleaning. Or maybe it's a quarterly task. You'll know best the maintenance process that works for you and the volume of data you create.

1
Information Overload

Unlike the clutter that fills our desk drawers and kitchen counters, digital clutter hides in plain sight. The amount of digital clutter we own is now limited only by storage capacity. And storage is cheap! The answer to digital clutter is NOT more digital storage. It's time to absorb what we've got, make decisions about how to filter it, and know where to find what's important.

At the genesis of this project, I had an insightful conversation with Hussein Janmohamed. He said, "We have to become masters of the digital world, or the digital world will rule us." The volume of information we are coping with (remember the 41.5 TB per household?) can easily take charge of our every moment unless we fight back.

1. Can You Stand the Noise?

Bosco Anthony, a leader in digital engagement, equated digital clutter to digital noise in his Social Media Camp presentation. Although silent, digital noise draws a lot of our attention.

The high volume of noise is a challenge. Every day we create and consume more information. From the first day of school photos to the newsfeeds from our preferred news channels plus social media posts and other entertainment content, there's so much to process.

In fact, the volume of data that needs to be processed exceeds our capacity. In his book, *The Art of Stillness* (Simon & Schuster, 2014), Pico Iyer comments on the problem, "… the more facts come streaming in on us, the less time we have to process any of them … the ability to gather information, which used to be so crucial, is far less important than the ability to sift through it." Iyer's observation is vital to our understanding of digital clutter. The more we have, the harder it is to find what we need to know or want to amuse us. Noisy beast!

Sadly, as we sift through information, we lose a bit of our humanity, too. The overwhelming volume deadens our emotional reactions, as we look at kitten photos followed by tragic world events one after the other. It also dulls our ability to think critically about what we are seeing. Perhaps worst of all, it renders us impotent when it's time to generate a proportional response, beyond a mere thumbs up or sad face icon. In essence, the digital noise deafens our capacity for compassion.

2. I Heard You but I Wasn't Listening

Too much is said that nobody pays any attention to. This era of social media is filled with people shouting just to hear the sound of their own voices. Are you truly listening? Have you found a way to overcome the challenge when there's too much to read, watch, or hear? With all that static, it's hard for each of us to tune into a particular voice. It's overwhelming and too often in this era of the digital life do we pretend to absorb some digital tidbit. But we don't fully absorb it unless we give it our full attention.

I think it's a two-sided problem. Content creators have to be judicious in what they share. Does it matter? Is it factual? Is it kind? It is helpful? No more purposeless noise, please. At the same time, listeners have to truly listen. What was said? How is it relevant? Is this truly an inspiration? Am I better informed?

My Mum had a great apology that I've adopted as my own. She would say "I'm sorry. I heard you but I wasn't listening." What distracted parent can't relate to that?

I love that she owned up to the fact that sometimes she wasn't really engaged in what I said. As a schoolteacher, her inner monologue would be filled with all sorts of problems and plans related to her classroom. Now that I, too, am a parent, I better understand that tricky transition time when it can be a struggle to shift from work gear to parent gear. The same is true online as we shift from social media to websites to financial reports. Sometimes the gear box is jammed!

All of us have this challenge in our technologically connected world. By decluttering our data, we can make it easier to commit to listening.

3. Develop Filters

Filters are an essential tool for sorting through digital clutter. We can use them to seek important information, auto-file reference information, and flag high-priority information.

At its most basic, you are the filter. With each piece of incoming information, you make a decision about what to do with it. You may choose to consume it, file it, or take action based on it. Of course, as the volume increases, more complex filters are needed and technology can help us filter.

Some use email rules for incoming messages. Your email program can likely be programmed to move messages automatically from your inbox to elsewhere. This can be done by the sender's name, a keyword in the subject, or some other tidbit of information embedded in the message. As an example, you might set up a rule to move any purchase receipts from iTunes or the Google Play store directly into your email archive.

Another type of filter is lists within social media accounts. These can be used to prioritize what you see. In Facebook, for example, it's common to have friend lists that group your close friends or acquaintances separately from groups of friends you self define such as parent group or prayer group. In another use, Twitter lists are helpful to organize people you follow according to topic so that your favorite restaurants, chefs, and foodies can be perused separately from your favorite teams and sports analysts. Select the list for the people or topics you want to read about at any given time.

Lists can be especially helpful when you have a time-limited social media session.

Another type of filter stops your web browser from accessing websites that can distract you from the task at hand. When you set them up, you select what websites you want to avoid while you're doing other things on your computer. For example, you might want to ignore news sites or social media sites. You can even have these apps block specific web pages or the Internet as a whole. The blocks are only in effect for the hours you also get to define. In an emergency, you can override the block; just be sure it's an emergency! If this type of filter is for you, try tools Self Control (Mac only), Cold Turkey (PC only), or Rescue Time (Mac or PC) to prevent distractions.

Even more complex filters can be built into workflow systems such as Slack or ToDoist that assign information to projects or processes. By assigning tasks to the correct person with the skills and knowledge to take action, other team members don't see the digital clutter unrelated to their contributions to the project.

Beyond the digital solutions, we may be seeking self-defined filters based on context. Finding ways to access data when and where we need reduces the "overwhelmed by information" feeling. The challenge is ensuring your travel details are accessible when you travel and less accessible when you're swapping political views on Twitter.

4. Fake News and Reliable Sources

Following the results of the 2016 US presidential election, the notion of "fake news" became mainstream. It highlighted that our collective ability to assess what is true and what is false has been detached from reality. However, the issue of fake news has existed in all media for decades and bias in the media has been an ongoing problem since the days of heralds in the town square. If you're not sure what I mean, peruse the extravagant headlines of the supermarket tabloids.

In some ways, it's simply easier to believe the authority that published the news. If it's in print (or audio or video) it must be true, right? However, we live in a time when anyone can be a publisher and news travels quickly without the benefit of fact checking.

Somewhere along the way our energy for critically analyzing what we've been told was depleted. I think this is part of the digital clutter problem. With so much to consume, it's hard to check every piece of information.

Adding to the problem is the notion of confirmation bias, our tendency to believe something that affirms what we want to hear. Similarly, the notion of repetition bias can also be a factor where repeated information becomes increasingly believable because we've heard it before. Both types of bias can be about politics or parenting or nutrition or any other subject. It takes less energy to absorb information that reinforces our existing perspective. In digital clutter terms, we tend to pick news sources and social media friends who share our point of view. However, we're doing ourselves a disservice by being ill informed about the opposing view.

We could debate that fake news is a blend of ignorance and apathy. Our education system may not have fully prepared us to think critically given the time and energy to do so. We may be exhausted from navigating a hectic world with little time for fact checking. While these things may be true, I'd argue that information overload adds to the problem. It's something to ponder as we contemplate our abundant data.

5. Spam, Duplicates, and Other Evils

Every digital citizen plays host to unwanted information. Spam email, browser tabs, duplicate files, and other bits of data clutter up our hard drives. Excessive notifications and oversubscribed email newsletter habits add to the problem.

Even robust spam filters let some sketchy messages reach our email inbox. Some are from smarmy spambots offering you fake coupons, unlikely inheritances, or medical miracles. Others are less obvious spam in the form of unrequested marketing offers, alumni benefits, or artificial networking invitations.

Browser tabs, bookmarks, and search histories can also haunt us. This self-inflicted digital clutter may be part of your workflow or a result of distractions while you're online. Too many tabs open can bring on tears if your browser crashes.

Copies are clutter that need to be banned unless they are part of a formal back-up plan. You, hopefully, have a method to back up your phone or laptop, ideally one that's automated. You'll only access this data if catastrophe strikes and you have to restore your information.

Notifications are a big evil when it comes to digital clutter. Notifications come from many sources: email, text messages, phone calls, social media, and more. The flags, beeps, and reminder pop-ups cut into your productivity and drive you to distraction.

These are just a few examples of unwanted information. As you explore your data, you'll declutter many different digital evils.

2
Technology Inventory

As we navigate the world as digital citizens, technology and data are everywhere.

Yet, we should be cautious in our definition of technology. In their time, the slate and pencil revolutionized education just as the steamship supercharged global immigration. The Trans-Canada Highway and the Amtrak network are also technological marvels largely taken for granted, yet so vital to the life experience of millions. Bridges, insulation, radio, and electric cars are each a technological marvel in their own right. In essence, technology is any mechanical innovation that changes the way we do something.

1. Shifts in Relationships with Technology

Starting in the late 1970s with the rise of the personal home computer, digital camera, and cellular phones, electronic technology became an increasing part of our daily lives. As more and more technology entered our homes for personal use our relationship with technology shifted, too. The speed of that shift increased exponentially around 2007 with the rise of social media and smartphones. Our information is increasingly filtered through technology and the devices themselves need to be managed. The quest to keep the cordless phone charged has evolved into a multi-device charging station in many homes and endless quests for an electrical outlet at the airport, shopping mall, or hospital.

As we refined how we lived with technology, many innovations were welcomed for their novelty, entertainment, or practical uses. The dazzle of convenience or fun had us adding technology as quickly as our budgets would allow. In some cases, the pace of innovation had us buying the same piece of technology over and over again. Cellular phones are an excellent example.

2. Taking Technology for Granted

However, too often, we take technology for granted. And, in some cases, we mistake technology's talents as a replacement for our own. Engida Gebre, an assistant professor in education technology at Simon Fraser University, noted in a recent lecture that "the computer is an extension of the mind. It's not a replacement." Technology in any form are tools that offer efficiency and access. However, those tools are only as useful as the person making use of them.

Unfortunately, we are dazzled by the bright shiny objects available to us. Sometimes, slavishly so with endless purchases of the latest mobile phone, laptop, or monitor. Smaller purchases slip in, too, as we are wooed by the advertising for new headphones, portable batteries, and other digital gadgetry. It doesn't take long to amass a massive collection of gadgets and gizmos.

3. Technology Collection Inventory

Decluttering your data requires a solid look at the technology in our lives. The things we use every day can stay. The special items that are still entertaining or useful can remain. But the clutter clearing starts with the useless tech objects that fill our lives. It's up to you, as much as you are able, to be honest about how much technology is cluttering your home or office.

Before you explore your digital clutter, it can be helpful to inventory your technology. Consider all that's in your home and your office and assess whether you still use it, even on occasion. Use the technology collection inventory available on the download kit to take stock as you read the rest of this chapter.

It may feel odd to start a digital cleanse by seeking your hardware. This is normal. However, data hides in surprising places. Having a clear idea of the technology you own will help you win when you play hide and seek with your data. As you fill in your inventory, leave in service items where you normally use them. At the same time, gather unused items in a central spot. I keep a box in my house to collect old technology. (More on what to do with the old stuff at the end of this chapter.)

The technology collection inventory includes commonly used categories of technology. Under each category make notes of what's in your collection. You'll also see some checkboxes. Use these to categorize your technology as "always," "sometimes," or "never" based on how you've used the device in the last 12 months.

3.1 Computers and peripherals

Computers come in many forms, from laptops to desktops plus servers and older netbooks. With every computer comes a myriad of peripherals including the keyboard, mouse, speakers, and monitors. Then there are the extras you may have such as a projector or docking station.

3.2 Phones and tablets

Mobile phones and landline handsets abound in most homes and offices. You may use the latest iOS or Android-enabled smartphone on an hourly basis but what about older models you've replaced? Don't forget you might have an ancient PalmPilot or Blackberry lingering in a drawer somewhere.

Tablets, too, have been around long enough for many of us to have more than one. Maybe you tried an iPad only to discover you prefer a Samsung tablet or vice versa. You may have upgraded to get a lighter, faster model that runs more recently developed apps. Or you may have a tablet tucked away that's so old the operating system won't boot anymore!

3.3 Gaming consoles and games

Gamers may use a computer but there are still lots of gaming consoles to choose from. PlayStation, Wii, or Xbox might have a home in your family room along with some smaller handheld game-focused devices such as the Nintendo 3DS. Add to that the games them-selves; some of which are still sold as cartridges. In addition, you may have older game licenses you may have purchased on CD-ROM.

3.4 E-readers

Depending on your position about reading paper versus bytes, your technology collection might include one or more e-readers. Every Kindle Paperwhite or Kobo Aura in your collection may have some forgotten ancestors gathering dust on your desk. Don't forget your tablet if you have a personal library on iBooks or Google Play Books.

3.5 Image, audio, and video equipment

If you're a content creator, filmmaker, or audiophile, your audio equipment may be taking up space. Microphones, mixers, pop fil-ters, and more can clutter your desk while SD cards in mobile re-corders can hide treasure troves of data. Similarly, DSLR cameras and video cameras can accumulate as older models are replaced by less weighty, higher resolution descendants. Don't forget about tripods, lighting, or other accessories that help you record.

3.6 Storage devices

Data storage is an ever-changing landscape and while the current standard is cloud computing, you've likely got some data hanging out in your office. Look for hard drives, SD cards, and USB sticks. Don't forget your PVR for all your broadcast television recordings. If you've been using computers for a long time, take a peek in your old zip drive and look for any lingering floppy disks.

3.7 Smart home devices

Smart home devices are a relatively new category so you may not have vast amounts to purge in this area. Take time to consider the smart features you've added to your home. Simple conveniences such as lightbulbs and thermostats may be tethered to your mo-bile phone. If you've renovated in recent years, you may also have bigger smart technology, too, so take a quick inventory of your appliances such as your refrigerator, washer, and dryer. Consider your security system, if you have one, and its connected cameras, sensors, and monitoring console.

3.8 Connectors

For most technology users, connecting cables, wires, and dongles seem to breed without human intervention. Every new device comes with one or more cables, many of which conform to the jacks on more than one piece of technology. Whether you have HDMI connectors, lightning cables, or other links, gather them for inspection.

Sample 2: Technology Collection Inventory

Note the technology in your life and how often you use it.

		Always	Sometimes	Never
Computers and peripherals	laptop	x		
	wireless keyboard		x	
	netbook			x
Phones and tablets	iPhone	x		
	iPad (wifi only)		x	
Gaming consoles and games	Xbox 360		x	
	Nintendo Switch	x		
	Nintendo 3DS			x
E-readers	Kindle		x	
	iBook (app)		x	
Image, audio, and video equipment	DSLR camera		x	
	audio recorder	x		
	lavalier microphone			x
Storage devices	assorted USB drives		x	
	external hard drive		x	

Sample 2 – Continued

Smart home devices	touchscreen fridge	x		
	light timers		x	
Connectors	HDMI cables		x	
	lightning cable	x		
Other	remote control droid			x
	wristband fitness tracker	x		

4. Repurpose, Donate, Recycle

Earlier in this chapter, I suggested you gather unused technology in a single location. When I first did this I was shocked by how much old tech was in my house. If you have some excess, too, it might be time to repurpose it, donate it, or send it to recycling. Some things may stay for nostalgia's sake and that's okay if it's a conscious decision.

So, what to do with that box full of old technology? First, contemplate whether or not you can repurpose something in your own home or office. Maybe an old computer is still powerful enough for a child's homework station. Or an unused mobile phone can become the bearer of the playlist in your car. Excessive cables can be wrangled by limiting yourself to one or two spares.

If you're certain you have no need to repurpose the technology in your home or office, then take a moment to consider if it contains any data. If so, hang on to it temporarily so you can deal with the information as part of your digital decluttering. If not, make some time to donate or recycle unwanted technology.

To donate technology, start within your own circle. Maybe a loved one or colleague would welcome something you're no longer using. Local charities may also accept functioning technology donations. For example, a shelter helping victims of abuse may be able to redistribute older model mobile phones. Another alternative may be a cooperative maker space, where your unwanted technology can be used by keen creators. Just be sure not to send any technology garbage to others. If it's unusable, take responsibility for disposal yourself.

I hope Free Geek, a nonprofit organization, will become a model for technology recycling. Volunteer-run locations accept donations of computers and related equipment, working or not, and refurbish them for donation or resale at nominal prices. In doing so, they make technology available to those who might not be able to afford retail prices. With locations in Portland, Chicago, Vancouver, Toronto, and elsewhere, tons of technology is finding a second life. Learn more at www.freegeek.org.

Disposing of electronics can be something of a headache. Some urban centers have centralized recycling programs where e-waste is processed separately from general refuse. Other communities don't have such facilities and technology ends up in the landfill. As much as possible, please be responsible with your technology garbage by removing any batteries and other parts that can be recycled in your community.

3
Digital Footprint

Like a mark in the sand, every piece of data connected to you leaves an impression on the Internet. I call this a digital footprint. Some details appear in search results while others hide on servers. Some are blatantly created on social media and others zing out of your email account. Still more are embedded in the technology you use every day. All of it collectively is part of your digital life.

1. Seeking Data

How do you define data? I think of data in two ways: created and passive. Created data is the information you consciously produce including emails and documents you write as well as videos and photographs you take. In contrast, passive data is the information you create by using technology. This includes things like your browsing history, credit card purchases, and Netflix "recently watched" list.

2. Digital Footprint Checklist

Let's take a closer look at your digital footprint. You might be surprised by all the things that contribute to your data. Some information is very visible such as your social media posts and text messages. Other data may have been set up and forgotten. And some details may be invisible to you.

As you read the rest of this chapter, use the digital footprint inventory in the workbook on the download kit to document elements of your digital footprint.

2.1 Internet access

How and where you get online is the first element of your digital footprint. This may include an Internet connection at home and another at the office. If you have a mobile phone, you may also pay for a data plan that keeps you connected when you're out and about. In addition, you may use public Internet access spots at a restaurant, shopping center, or other public place.

Even with privacy settings turned on and location services turned off, you leave behind digital footprints that note your approximate location and the type of device you're using. You may also pick up some tracking pixels or cookies, tiny bits of code websites used to track your visits, not the delicious kind from the local bakery.

2.2 Servers

Servers are another aspect of your digital footprint. They facilitate your access to the Internet and house your data. Your email runs through a server, too. It's increasingly common for families to have a media server where they can share all their music, television, and movies. Servers are essential to our use of the Internet but they are also part of your digital footprint.

Your home or office may include one or more servers. Do you have access? Are you in control? Or do you work through a system administrator who takes care of the technical details behind the scenes?

Typically, it's only the loss of access to a server that highlights how dependent we are on this aspect of our digital footprint. If the server goes down, it will impact your access to information and your ability to communicate. A formal system administrator may solve the problem. If you use a home-based server, be clear on who has control. After a power failure, someone has to log your family back on when the server resets.

2.3 Websites

Websites don't appear in some people's digital footprint and make up a huge part of others'. Take a moment to consider all the websites you own, if any. Be sure to add any websites you contribute to even if you don't own them.

Content is the most visible part of your website including text, photos, audio, video, and more. Add to that smaller details such as categories, tags, and links. All of these elements are part of the digital footprint.

Behind the scenes that footprint expands to include domain registry, web hosting, and any related subscription services. If all functions well, these aspects are invisible. But when something breaks they become critical.

2.4 Email and databases

Email is a huge part of most people's digital footprint. Home accounts, school accounts, and work accounts, plus any lingering defunct email addresses house a lot of data. Your inbox and sent items combined with any filed or archived messages can result in gigabytes of data. The longer you've used an email account, the more data it holds. Whether you use Gmail or a custom server, odds are the volume of email you own is massive.

Add to this the marketing tools that facilitate email list services. Companies such as AWeber, Constant Contact, and MailChimp help businesses gather email addresses for marketing purposes. Sometimes businesses use a customer relationship management tool such as Raiser's Edge or Infusionsoft to collect information beyond email.

These robust systems also track participation, purchase histories, and other notes related to the business's relationship with the individual. If you are a business owner, you may have such a system. As an individual your information is likely housed in such a system at several businesses and/or charities.

2.5 Storage solutions

Where you store your digital information adds to your digital footprint. This might include a hard drive on your computer and the memory in your mobile phone. Don't forget the data on older computers, tablets, and mobile phones; odds are you have several hiding in closets and drawers around your home or office. Or they've been handed on to children or others in your circle who use hand-me-down technology.

Depending on your workflow, you may also have data stored on USB drives, SD cards, and other small, portable memory devices. SD cards, for example, continue to be the standard for digital SLR cameras. You likely also have some older data stored such as on CD, Blu-ray or, going way back, floppy disk.

Current solutions typically include cloud storage. You may be using services such as iCloud, Google Drive, Dropbox, or similar to make your data accessible on multiple devices. The convenience of cloud storage makes for great workflow but it adds to our digital footprint as those clouds are really massive servers housed in major civic centers, most often in the United States.

Whatever storage solutions work for you, make notes on your digital footprint inventory.

2.6 Productivity services

As our working lives become increasingly mobile, our work tools become increasingly digital. Whether you work for a big company or as a solo entrepreneur, you'll access information and communicate with colleagues through your computer.

Communication by instant messenger and email are common. Video chat and virtual phones are often used. Collaborative workflow may be facilitated through an internal ticketing system or a productivity tool such as BaseCamp or Slack. In addition to the desktop versions of these programs, you may also have an app on your mobile phone that keeps you connected to the office.

Digital calendars are also the norm with information syncing in real time between your computer, tablet, and mobile phone. Shared calendars allow that information to be distributed amongst family members and work colleagues, as appropriate.

2.7 Social media and online communities

Our next category is social media. Depending on how you use social networks, this could be a big part of your digital footprint.

As an individual, you may have accounts on Facebook, You-Tube, Instagram, LinkedIn, and Twitter. If you have friends and family outside North America, you may also have accounts on VK (Russia), RenRen (China), Orkut (Brazil), or any one of dozens of other non-English social networks. You may also have accounts on one of the lesser known sites such as 500PX, a professional photography community, or Ravelry, a community for those who knit or crochet. In fact, there are thousands of social networks serving special interest communities.

> As you gather details of your digital footprint, you'll notice you've got a long list of usernames with passwords. Knowing how to log in to your various accounts is another way to reduce your digital footprint. Don't waste time and clutter your email resetting your passwords every time you have a memory lapse.
>
> To keep track of your logins, save the information in a safe place. Some people still use a notebook to track this information which works well unless the notebook is lost or the paper is damaged by a spilled cup of coffee. A spreadsheet is another frequently used alternative. For a digital solution that manages your passwords for you, look at services such as 1Password (https://1password.com), Dashlane (www.dashlane.com), or LastPass (www.lastpass.com). The service remembers all your passwords so you don't have to memorize them. They generate long and complex passwords that are hard for hackers to crack and all you have to remember is one key password.

Beyond your personal accounts, you may control or contribute to business accounts on social media. This may mean a Facebook page, separate from your Facebook profile, plus business accounts on Instagram, Twitter, LinkedIn, and other sites. The professional social digital footprint can grow even further if a company has a social media presence for various locations or a variety of branded products.

2.8 Shopping accounts

If you have embraced online shopping, you know the convenience and complexities of wish lists, shopping carts, payments, and shipping instructions. Each element of the experience adds to our digital footprint and the things we buy adds to the clutter in our homes. Dealing with the purchases is another kind of decluttering!

Online shoppers have a wide range of vendor options to buy virtual and physical goods. Movies, music, and television shows are available as fast as we can download them through iTunes, Google Play, and other vendors. Clothes, books, food, and housewares can be quickly ordered from general stores such as Amazon or brand-specific stores; one of my favorites is Lands' End.

We may also shop for services when we book accommodations through Airbnb or VRBO or arrange for a ride with Lyft or Uber. Sometimes in-person services such as a spa appointment can be booked and paid for online so there's no need to fuss with money at the spa. We can also purchase and send digital gift cards and reload our favorite cards through PayPal or a dedicated app such as the one used to order your next cup of coffee at Starbucks.

With every purchase, we add to our digital footprint. The vendor gets our details as does the shipping company. If you should buy from another country, a common occurrence for Canadians interested in American brands, there are also often duties and taxes to pay.

2.9 Loyalty programs and memberships

Another element of our digital footprint comes from loyalty programs. A close ally of online shopping, loyalty programs generate and collect data about us both online and in-store.

Rite Aid wellness+ points and Shoppers' Drug Mart Optimum points can be exchanged for free drugstore products. Similarly, your points on fuel purchases can be cashed in to collect road snacks at the convenience store or for free gas. Simply use your Esso Extra, Exxon Plenti, or a similar card for your preferred brand of fuel, to earn points for every purchase. Travelers can also collect loyalty points. Depending on where you fly you may collect Qantas Points or WestJet Dollars.

Other programs allow you to collect points at a variety of merchants. AIR MILES is a good example. With an AIR MILES collector number you can make purchases at stores for home improvement, gas, groceries, and at many other retailers all while collecting points towards a single rewards system.

Sometimes you don't have to join a formal points program. Michaels, the craft superstore, for example, simply uses customers' email addresses to track purchases, send discount coupons, and advertising offers. The more store visits and larger volume of purchases made, the higher the discount coupons offered.

Beyond loyalty programs, you may also have memberships to consider. Professional associations, gym memberships, buying clubs, and other memberships all add to your digital footprint.

No matter what loyalty programs or memberships you select, it's important to be aware that all of these programs collect data about customers. They reward loyal customers with perks such as discounts, free products, and exclusive offers. However, each piece of information they gather contributes to big data about shopping habits and so on. Something to keep that in mind next time you sign up.

2.10 Online banking

Most of our money lives in a digital place. Even though your bank or credit union might have brick and mortar locations, the bills and coins on hand are a miniscule part of financial systems. All financial records are stored digitally including checking and savings accounts, credit cards, loans, and retirement funds. In addition, it is common to do some virtual banking through PayPal, Square, or proprietary shopping carts with various vendors. Those digital records include details on each transaction including location and time stamps.

If you own a business, you may also have responsibility for sales transactions, related income, and any affiliate programs you are part of. An affiliate program may involve you collecting money for sales of items for which you earn income or dispensing money to pay vendors selling your products. If you have staff members or contractors, you'll have the added financial complications of payroll, retirement contributions, tax withholdings, and other deductions.

2.11 Gaming accounts

Online gaming has millions of participants globally. Government sanctioned gambling, subscriptions on aggregate gaming services such as STEAM and individual accounts with Roblox, World of Warcraft, and others all add to your digital footprint. In addition, you may invest in apps for your iOS or Android phone that include memberships or a centralized gaming hub. Often these games invite you to connect through Facebook or another social network with friends who are also players. Each game adds to your digital footprint.

Within many games, in-game purchases help enhance your experience. In some cases, they allow you to succeed more quickly. In other cases, purchases unlock additional elements of the game. Either way the records of in-game purchases extend your digital footprint even more.

2.12 Entertainment accounts

Separate from gaming, are the accounts that entertain us with movies, television, music, and things to read. Depending where you are in the world, you may have access to one or more subscription services such as Netflix, Vudu, Hulu, CBS All Access, or other services to watch television and movies.

Similarly, many magazines offer digital editions through online accounts. A wide range are also available from Texture, one of my favorite accounts, which is essentially Netflix for magazines. If books are of interest you may also have a paid service such as Kindle Unlimited or a library ebook loan such as Overdrive.

Music subscriptions come in a range of options from Spotify to Apple Music. Music albums can also be purchased as can single songs.

All of these accounts track what you've watched, listened to, and read. That information is used to add to big data about buying patterns and to customize future offers for you. Check your recommendations on Netflix, as an example. Every entertainment account you have adds to your digital footprint.

2.13 Events and tickets

Ticketed events can also add to your digital footprint. Whether you go to see motivational speakers, the local sports team, or your favorite band, you likely purchased your ticket online through a service such as Ticketmaster or Eventbrite.

Depending on how many events you choose to attend, you may have a long list of past and future events on your calendar and the records of your corresponding ticket purchases.

In addition, consider your event host status. Are you planning events that have digital records? If you've created a guest list, playlist, or booked a caterer, there's a digital footprint.

2.14 Medical attention

Depending where you live, access to medical services can be a challenge. In urban areas, you may have several potential clinics or hospitals nearby but those in rural areas have less choice. If you live with socialized medicine, you can go to the closest location but those living with a privatized system or with complex insurance coverage may have less choice if they want their medical expenses covered.

Regardless of the medical system, when you need medical attention, digital records improve communication amongst caregivers: Records from the blood clinic, immunization records, x-rays, and other tests. Access to your medical history can streamline treatment if you have a chronic or complex condition that has already been thoroughly investigated.

Your digital footprint may also include the opportunity to hear test results by video chat with your doctor through Live Care or a similar app, saving the trouble of a trip to the clinic or having to take time off work to go to the doctor's clinic during office hours.

Medical finances also add to your digital footprint. Centralized services, medical aid, and insurance accounts all have log-ins and records of your trips to the clinic, lab, and hospital.

2.15 Academic interfaces

Every student from kindergarten to university has an academic digital footprint. School records include grades, standardized testing, and class placements as well as emergency contact information, health records, and any disciplinary actions.

As students get older, their classes may include virtual learning. Colleges and universities operate through systems such as Canvas or Desire to Learn (D2L). Meanwhile, continuing education and lifelong learning courses may be offered through systems such as Thinkific or Webinar Jam. Within these systems, students can access course files, reading material, video tutorials, online discussions, and assignments. Peer and instructor feedback can also be communicated.

Once schooling is complete, there may also be alumni activities. Social events to professional networking opportunities, continued access to the college library, or other perks are all facilitated by digital access.

As you can see, our digital footprint hides in a wide variety of activities. The Digital Footprint inventory (see Sample 3) provides a snapshot of the digital clutter in your life today. Throughout *Declutter Your Data* we're going to talk about a blend of these digital categories. Some will apply to your situation more than others. On occasion, I'll focus on specific types but be aware that you can adapt the advice throughout the book to data as it appears in your life.

Sample 3: Digital Footprint Inventory

Make notes on the digital elements of your life to better explore your digital clutter.

Internet access	high-speed broadband, 3GB/month cellular data
Servers	home-media server
Websites	none
Email and databases	angela@angelacrocker.com, Constant Contact
Storage solutions	Google Drive, Dropbox, iCloud
Productivity services	Slack, Evernote

Sample 3 – Continued

Social media and online communities	Facebook, Instagram, LinkedIn, Twitter, school PAC
Shopping accounts	Lands' End, ThinkGeek, Amazon Prime
Loyalty programs and memberships	wellness+ points, AIR MILES
Online banking	credit union, bank
Gaming accounts	Steam, Roblox, Game Center
Entertainment accounts	Netflix, Hulu, Texture
Events and tickets	Ticketmaster, Eventbrite, Cineplex, local concert hall
Medical attention	MedicAlert, travel medical insurance
Academic interfaces	Canvas, Lynda.com, Skillshare
Other	

4

The Myth of a Perfect Life

Digital living has created a self-perpetuating myth that we all have to live with. The illusion of the perfect life is easily cultivated by carefully curating the public elements of our digital footprint. The tendency is to put our best face forward, never telling the hard truths, and sharing a palatable, edited version of reality. This polished version of life can protect privacy yet it also lacks real moments and impedes our opportunities for genuine connections.

In Sophie Kinsella's novel *My Not So Perfect Life*, (The Dial Press, 2017), the friction between protagonist, Katie Brenner, and her boss, Demeter Farlowe, creates a rollicking tale of misunderstandings. The moral of the story is simply "Why did you believe my [digital] hype when you knew your own hype was all fiction?" It's such a truism.

Perpetuating the myth of a perfect life has far reaching consequences. Loss of self-esteem, digital addiction, social stress, extreme fatigue, overspending, and other issues can result. These impacts are very real and an important part of why it's essential to take charge of our data and organize our digital lives.

1. In Consideration of Minimalism

When I talk about digital decluttering, I'm not speaking from a minimalist's point of view. I like my things; physical and digital. However, my practice aligns with the minimalist movement in that I think we should only keep what's purposeful or joyful. I like what Francine Jay, also known as Miss Minimalist, says about minimalism in her book *The Joy of Less* (Anja Press, 2010). She writes:

"Most people hear the word 'minimalism' and think 'empty.' Unfortunately, 'empty' isn't altogether appealing; it's usually associated with loss, deprivation, and scarcity. But look at 'empty' from another angle — think about what it is instead of what it isn't — and now you have 'space.' Space! That's something we could all use more of! Space in our closets, space in our garages, space in our schedules, space to think, play, create, and have fun with our families ... now that's the beauty of minimalism."

Digital declutter can be reduced, even minimized, to create mental and digital space for other things. This can counterattack the social pressures of the elusive perfect life and free us to focus on the digital things that matter most, customized to our own priorities.

2. Defending Conversation

In a digital life, conversation is both an opportunity and a challenge.

On the one hand, you can send messages by text, audio, or video to stay connected with family, friends, and colleagues. If they are online at the same time, a conversation can continue in real time. If they happen to be offline, your message is still delivered and awaits their response closing the gaps of time zones and geography.

On the other hand, the art of conversation may be getting lost in the digital clutter. Text messages and emojis fail to deliver the nuances of facial expression, vocal inflection, and eye contact. Context can also be lost when the sender and receiver are unaware of one another's circumstances. The message "I'm sad" takes on different meanings when sent from an ICU waiting room in contrast with an athlete's courtside communique. Again, the myth of a perfect life pops up when we lose this context.

Changing our digital conversations into face-to-face chats may also increase understanding and make dialogue productive. As Jessica Martin wrote in *Teen Vogue,* (Volume 1, 2017), "By putting down the phone, we're opening up the window for real dialogue ... in-person discussions, especially about controversial issues, are much more productive."

As an experiment, challenge yourself to a month of daily conversations. Set aside distractions and focus on one person at a time in conversation each day. Talk to your grandmother, your assistant, your neighbor. See what truths about their realities you can learn. To note your progress, use the Conversation Challenge Tracker to give yourself a sticker reward for each conversation and, if you like, note the length of the chat. At the end of the month, tally up how many hours you spent connecting with the people in your life and reflect on its impact. (See Sample 4.)

3. The Costs of Digital Living

Digital living is an expense. The technology we buy. The accessories we add-on. The software we purchase. The content we consume. Every element has a price tag and those costs can add up very quickly. The amount we have to spend may influence how we are perceived.

To access all the latest digital living has to offer, the expenditures are the same for every individual no matter their income. Yet income varies widely and alters the choices available to each person. Most people can't afford a $1,000 device every year so your laptop, tablet, or mobile phone, if you have them, may be two or more years old. Similarly, some digital citizens can't afford to buy all the ebooks they want to read so they rely on a lending library instead.

Beyond money, there is also a cost in terms of attention and productivity. How you choose to spend your time and focus is vital to everyday life. PhD researcher Nicole Johnson noted, "My productivity has increased enormously now that I'm spending more time offline." For others, time spent online can increase productivity by reducing travel or streamlining communication. Either way, be aware of any nonmonetary costs.

Sample 4: Conversation Challenge Tracker

As part of the daily conversation challenge, give yourself a sticker reward and note the number of minutes of conversation each day. Tally your minutes for the month.

Date: January 25 – February 22

Sunday	Monday	Tuesday	Wednesday	Thursday	Friday	Saturday
⭐ 20	⭐ 10	⭐ 30	⭐ 10	⭐ 20		⭐ 10
⭐ 10	⭐ 30	⭐ 10	⭐ 20		⭐ 10	⭐ 40
⭐ 30	⭐ 10	⭐ 20		⭐ 10	⭐ 30	⭐ 40
⭐ 20	⭐ 10		⭐ 30	⭐ 20	⭐ 10	⭐ 20

Total minutes: 470 (about 8 hours)

Reflections on conversation:

I enjoyed my conversation throughout the month.

I learned news from several friends about things they wouldn't share online.

I feel more connected to friends and family.

I did well with conversations 24 out of 28 days. I'll try again for 100%.

For some, the cost of digital living is an unavoidable expense in order to conduct business and earn an income. For others, technology is a playground for entertainment with a long menu of optional amusement expenses. Next time you buy technology or a piece of content, contemplate whether that new mobile phone or game is a toy or a tool.

> There's another hidden cost in digital living and it's paid by the content creators. Many books, songs, and movies are available for illegal download. While these services make the content available to a wide audience, there are ethical considerations when the content creators are not compensated. Next time you're looking at a bootleg download, take a moment to think about who pays the content creators.

Sadly, some members of society are superficial enough to pass judgment. I hold out hope for a utopian future where the amount we spend has less influence on how we are perceived. Does an older model mobile phone label you as frugal or out of fashion? It depends who you ask. And this problem adds to the myth of digital living.

4. The Privilege of Digital Access

We live in extraordinary times where technology and digital access abound. The speed of connectivity, the variety of digital creations, and the incredible volume of information available are mind boggling. However, digital access is a privilege. *BC Bookworld* highlighted the issue in its Spring 2017 article "Storming the Digital Divide: The PovNet Story." In this article it is said, "It is nowadays taken for granted, especially by younger people, that nearly everyone knows about the Internet and how to access it. This assumption can be crippling to someone who has never been familiar with a keyboard, or who can't afford an iPhone, or who still doesn't know what the heck an 'app' is."

Access to technology, digital literacy, and content to consume are not available to all. And some who have access may not fully understand what to do with the technology, how to participate in the digital conversation, or where to find content that suits their budget. Others may have partial access with occasional connectivity at the library or community center. At all times, those with full access should be aware of these individuals and think carefully about whether or not they want to perpetuate the myth of the perfect life.

5. An Integrated Digital Life

In my view, we all need to live an integrated digital life; one where we embrace the best of both digital and analog experiences. Finding the right balance will, to some extent, depend on our access to technology and content. It also depends on our appetite for gadgets and digital entertainment. If digital is part of your life, then you need to find the blend that works for you.

Think of it as making a cup of tea. Brew a weak cup and you have too little digital in your life; something is missing. Yet, brew a strong cup and suddenly you have too much digital; your life is cluttered and overwhelmed. The perfect cup is unique to your taste and includes the digital elements that contribute to your productivity, social connections, and happiness.

If you'd like ongoing support in building your integrated digital life, I invite you to tune into my podcast, "It's a Digital Life." The show is designed to talk about the issues, challenges, and joys of living a digital life. If you'd like to tune in, visit www.angelacrocker. com/podcast.

We no longer live completely offline nor strictly online. As Ian Sherr wrote in *CNET* magazine, "It's almost impossible to detach ourselves from the digital world these days." ("Get Off Your Phone," Fall 2017). There is often talk about the balance between digital to analog. Rather than thinking of them as exclusive extremes, I suggest we look at them as end points on a pendulum in motion.

As we move through each day, we swing through various points on the pendulum. At one end of the arc, we may be fully analog using fine art supplies in a journal. At the other end, we might be fully digitally engaged in a video conference call. In between, we may take our fitness playlist and heart monitor on a run through the local trails.

This integrated digital life needs regular maintenance. Once established, digital and analog priorities have to be reevaluated from time to time. As Vicki McLeod wrote in her book *#Untrending*, (Main Street Communications, 2016), "There is life beyond the polarity of online or offline. It is the world we inhabit together. To know it requires us to slow down and pay attention. If we don't, we'll miss the moments that matter."

You may adjust seasonally with more Netflix binge nights in the cold of winter and more tech-free swimming in summer. You also have to resist outside influences or, at least, be alert to them.

We have to make choices about what we use and what to do that make sense for our priorities. Not everyone will share your priorities and they may try to adjust your balance without permission. It's up to you whether you adapt or resist those influences.

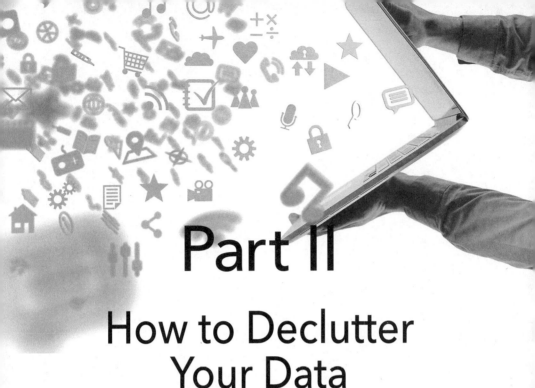

Part II

How to Declutter Your Data

Fortunately, there are many ways to wrangle digital clutter. In some cases, you may have more data than you realized. No matter what kind of clutter you have, you will find techniques in this section to help you take charge of your digital footprint. Some involve looking at your own behavior including your response times, privacy decisions, offline vacation plans, and digital physical fitness. Others look at the way you access and organize information including turning off notifications, digital calendars, email management, photo storage, and estate planning. Overall, your goal in this section is to identify and apply the strategies that help mold your unique digital footprint. Read on to learn how to declutter your data.

5
Your Digital Report Card

Now that you've got some sense of what digital clutter is, why digital decluttering is important to you, and the places to look for it, let's turn our attention to what to do about it. It's time to take action.

In the chapters that follow, I've mapped out practical tasks and an assortment of experience-based advice to help you tackle your digital clutter. I've sequenced these chapters to give you some easier tasks to warm up on before we get to the heavy lifting of email and estate planning.

Declutter in my suggested sequence or mix it up in an order that works for you. Either way, you'll be taking meaningful steps to organize your information and reduce your digital footprint.

To help you see your progress, I've created a digital report card for you to complete. You'll find a blank report card in the download kit included with this book. (See Sample 5.)

As you can see in Sample 5, I've included all of the categories of digital clutter that come in the chapters that follow. Start by giving yourself a grade for each category. For your first set of grades

Sample 5: Digital Report Card

This is your digital report card. Give yourself a letter grade for each category of digital clutter. Check back at regular intervals to reassess your grades and note your progress.

Date:	May 9	July 15		
Just say no	B	A		
Response time	C	B		
Notifications	B	B		
Dedicated devices	N/A	C		
Digital calendar	C	A		
App diet	D	B		
Consolidate your data	C	B		
Email	F	C		
Photos & videos	C	C		
Smart home	N/A	N/A		
Privacy	D	A		
Connections	B	B		
Social networks	B	B		
Digital vacation	D	C		
Pursue your passions	B	B		
Fake news	A	B		
Ideas	B	A		
Digital parenting	N/A	N/A		
Estate planning	D	C		
Librarian	B	B		
Physical fitness	C	B		
Priorities	1. Privacy	1. Photos	1.	1.
	2. Email	2. Estate	2.	2.
	3. Photos	3. Vacation	3.	3.
Notes				

go with your gut instinct. As you assess your data in more detail, scores can rise and fall according to your progress. Just like in school, use these familiar letter grades:

- A means your data in this area is in excellent condition: Nothing to declutter and you're happy with what you've got.

- B means your data in this area is in good condition: There's a bit to do but nothing that's pressing.

- C means your data in this area is average condition: It's not a disaster but it could be better.

- D means your data is in poor condition: Your files are in tough shape and it's going to take a lot of work to get them back on track.

- F means your data is a disaster: It's in such a mess that you're having trouble knowing where to start.

- N/A means not applicable: Either you have no data in this category or you've decided to exclude a category from your digital cleanse.

On the digital report card, there are four columns for you to check in with your digital decluttering progress. To track five or more check-ins, print additional copies from the download kit included with this book. Use the first column for your pre-declutter check-in. Fill in the other columns at regular intervals to build a snapshot of your progress. The time interval is up to you. Some people might check in monthly while others do it quarterly. There's no set time frame. Feel free to work at your own pace.

At the bottom of each column on your digital report card is a priorities list. Use this space to note your top three priorities when it comes to digital decluttering. Hopefully, you'll make progress between one check in and the next. As Vicki McLeod wrote in her book *#Untrending,* "Figure out your priorities and do things that support your priorities first." Of course, Vicki was writing about broader life priorities and I support you finding time for those in cooperation with your digital decluttering objectives.

Note that your priorities should change over time. If one priority keeps lingering on the list, reflect on what's stopping you from accomplishing that goal.

6
Just Say No

As you begin your digital decluttering journey, the ability to say no is a foundational skill. You can use it to stop digital clutter before it begins. Try it out to limit the number of online shopping carts, loyalty programs, and gaming accounts. Accounts you don't open create no digital clutter.

In categories where you must say yes, limit yourself to the minimum possible number. If you're seeking credit solutions, apply for one credit card, not six. If you're in need of concert tickets, buy from a centralized box office, not each individual venue. If you're making charitable donations, contribute larger amounts to fewer charities to reduce the related digital clutter.

Wherever possible, simplify your digital footprint. Say no to the excess with one account, fewer email addresses, or anything else you can limit.

1. How to Say No

We all have the opportunity to say no, but many forget this is an option. Getting to say no is a choice. It may help to practice. Say "no" now. There's great power in that two letter word. You can use it to save time, declutter your data, free up your calendar, and reduce your reading list. Model these sentences:

- No, thank you, I don't want to join your email list.

- No, I don't need to save this 46 GB video clip.

- No, I'm not going to sign up for another webinar.

- No, children, you can't have more screen time today.

- No, I decline your shopper's loyalty program.

See how that works? It's powerful, right? As Julie Cole said at the national Mompreneur™ Canada conference, "'No' is a complete sentence." Use it often. Use it wisely.

You can use that power to say no to new social networks. For example, do you Snapchat? You don't have to. Sure, social media marketing gurus tell you it's the latest and greatest thing, and it might turn out to be huge, but you don't have to be an early adopter (unless perhaps you are a social media marketing guru). You can say no. If at some later date you realize Snapchat is ideal for your project or business model, then go ahead and change that "no" to a "yes."

2. The Value of Your Time

Using "no" successfully requires you to be clear on your current priorities. Your focus at the office, your family's needs, and your relaxation efforts will all take priority at various times. And we know there is a limited amount of time to devote to each activity.

Remember, each day you have 86,400 seconds to spend. You get to decide how to spend them. Every "no" frees up seconds for something else that fits your priorities. Keep your time in perspective. Each day on average you'll use:

- 24,300 seconds to sleep

- 7,200 seconds to commute

- 5,400 seconds to eat

- 3,600 seconds to exercise

- 2,700 seconds to shower

43,200 seconds remain. That's 12 hours. How will you spend your time? To help you figure that out, the workbook on the download kit includes a Time Tracker Worksheet. Each week at a glance lets you visualize how you're spending your time both online and offline. Try tracking what you do over the next week and see if your priorities and your time management are in alignment. (See Sample 6.)

3. Habit Making

Another aspect of saying "no" is to build habits that support "no." You can do this in your home and in your office. Here are some habits you could cultivate in support of an integrated digital life:

- Establish tech-free zones. At home this might be the bedroom or bathroom. At the office, create an analog meeting space.

- Set up tech-free times. As a family, you might agree that all devices are turned off from 10:00 a.m. to 12:00 p.m. daily. At the office, have your team agree that no one reads, replies, or sends any emails on Friday afternoons.

- Impose a digital curfew. Turn off all family devices from 10:00 p.m. to 7:00 a.m. daily. If you use a work-only mobile, turn it off outside office hours.

- Store your mobile phone in another room or your briefcase. If it's not immediately at hand, you won't check it as often.

- Set up times to check notifications for social media, email, and other communication. This could be once a day, three times a day, or hourly. More or less is acceptable, too, depending on the type of digital life you want.

- Agree to one or more meals without technology. Try tech-free family breakfasts or dinners. At the office, have a weekly tech-free brown-bag lunch for your whole team.

- Take mini-breaks without social media. Chat with those around you instead of checking Facebook in the grocery store checkout line.

- Be present with the people around you. Don't check your phone in the middle of a conversation.

Sample 6: Time Tracker Worksheet

Map out your priorities to see if your activities align with your priorities both online and offline.

	Sunday	Monday	Tuesday	Wednesday	Thursday	Friday	Saturday
12:00 a.m.	sleep	sleep	sleep	sleep	sleep	sleep	sleep
1:00 a.m.							
2:00 a.m.							
3:00 a.m.							
4:00 a.m.							
5:00 a.m.							
6:00 a.m.							
7:00 a.m.		wake-up routine	wake-up routine	wake-up routine	wake-up routine	wake-up routine	
8:00 a.m.	wake-up routine	podcast commute	ebook commute	podcast commute	ebook commute	podcast commute	wake-up routine
9:00 a.m.		work email	work email	work email	work email	work email	social media
10:00 a.m.	digital vacation day	project work	team meeting	project work	project work	project work	unplugged family time
11:00 a.m.							
12:00 p.m.							
1:00 p.m.		work email	work email	work email	work email	work email	
2:00 p.m.	fitness	project work	project work	project work	finance meeting	project work	fitness
3:00 p.m.							
4:00 p.m.							
5:00 p.m.		podcast commute	ebook commute	podcast commute	ebook commute	podcast commute	family pizza and movie night
6:00 p.m.	family time	unplugged family time	night school course	fitness	unplugged family time	unplugged family time	
7:00 p.m.							
8:00 p.m.				unplugged family time			
9:00 p.m.							
10:00 p.m.	bedtime routine	social media	social media	social media	social media	bedtime routine	bedtime routine
11:00 p.m.		bedtime routine	bedtime routine	bedtime routine	bedtime routine	sleep	sleep

- Connect in person with someone you talk to online. Maybe someone you know well, or take a chance to get better acquainted with an acquaintance.

Building new habits can be hard. I suggest you start with one or two and stick with them for a month or so before adding more.

Use digital support or analog solutions, as appropriate. If you need a little extra help, set reminders to unplug. Make it an unbreakable appointment. Try the Disney Circle device to block Internet access to your technology (https://meetcircle.com/) or use a blocker app to temporarily hide websites that distract you. Invest in an old-school alarm clock so you don't need your mobile phone or tablet by the bed.

Whatever habits you establish should be designed to set boundaries around your digital use. By stepping away you will be more productive and effective in those hours when you are online.

7
Establish Your Response Time

Establishing your response time is key to a sane digital life. As you're reading this book, I think it's safe to assume you want more calm than chaos. Let's say you have four active social media accounts. In addition to posting your own content, you'll need to reply and follow up with your friends, fans, and followers. In order to do that effectively, you need to have a firm grasp on your response time.

1. How Fast Is Fast Enough?

How fast you reply may depend on whether it's a personal interaction or a business response. Personal interactions can happen in your leisure time or during your bus commute. Friends and family understand that you may be at work and unavailable much of the day.

Business responses are different. In some cases, the client expects an instant reply. In other cases, you've got a bit of time but how fast is fast enough? If you respond instantly, you must have a workflow that can tolerate constant interruptions. Is your topic time sensitive? If not, sending a response within a few hours may be perfectly reasonable to your clients. They know you're busy working for them (or other clients) and they want you to be focused and doing a great job.

If you respond within a day, I think that's the outside limit for an acceptable response for business purposes. Respond within one business day, if at all possible. If you only respond when you remember to check or when you have time or when you feel like it, I suggest you need to rethink being in business. Looking after your customers has to be a priority. Worst of all is no response at all. How does that make your clients feel? Will they want to do business with you? Of course, not. You are at risk of losing a customer to a competitor.

2. What's Your Response Time Going to Be?

I encourage you to make a decision on your response time and be consistent with it. Fans and followers will grow accustomed to hearing from you in a certain interval. For business, you may choose to respond within a few hours on weekdays and less frequently on weekends. Personal replies may be more or less frequent. With personal connections, you might respond to social media three times a day: early morning, after lunch, and evening. At a minimum, I'll be responding three times a day.

Admittedly, weekend response times are less structured as I integrate any weekend work into family time. (See Sample 7.)

3. Respond to Everything?

One last thing: Social media is about conversation and building relationships. It's about being present and part of what's happening. When you're in response mode, respond to as many people as you can. And know that it's OK when the conversation fizzles. Face-to-face conversations do that, too.

Sample 7: Response Time Planner

Note the frequency and interval of your intended response times.

	Personal	Business
Monday	Check personal email and social media morning and evening.	Check work email at 9 a.m. and 1 p.m. each business day.
Tuesday		
Wednesday		
Thursday		
Friday		
Saturday	Check social media throughout the day. Chat with friends.	No work-related responses on weekends.
Sunday	Digital vacation day.	

Notes

8
Turn off Notifications

Notifications come in many different modes. Your computer or mobile phone might beep, vibrate, pop-up a notice, or display a notification flag. Notifications distract you from your current task, ruin your productivity, and create stress. As Adam Gazzaley and Larry D. Rosen noted in their book *The Distracted Mind* (The MIT Press, 2016), "We can no longer focus in the classroom or the workplace; nor can we resist the pull of responding to alerts and notifications while we are supposed to be spending time with our family and friends."

In general, I advise you turn off audible and vibrating notifications for all of your mobile and desktop applications. Audible and vibrating notifications, in particular, drive many people crazy! *Bing. Bing. Bing. Buzz. Buzz. Buzz.* Frankly, in public, your notifications are a distraction to everyone around you. Good manners in this digital era include not disrupting others with unnecessary noise. Let's all make sure our notifications aren't at fault.

Visual notifications can also be a distraction so consider turning those off, too. However, it can be useful to have notification flags turned on to draw your attention to new content or responses that need your attention. For example, you may keep flag notifications turned on in Facebook. However, you can prevent the distracting element of notifications by only opening a browser tab (or the app) for Facebook when you have time to interact on this social network.

1. But I Need to Know What's Happening

Everyone has their own preferences for monitoring social accounts, email, and other incoming digital information. Some keep active tabs open in a browser. Others use a social media dashboard such as Hootsuite or AgoraPulse. Still others prefer to have mobile apps on their home screen and notifications turned on.

In most tools you can custom set the notification flags you'll see. Maybe you want alerts for new likes, comments, and friend requests but don't need notifications for marketing messages and coupon offers. Once set, the flags you'll see are only for the notifications you want to receive.

The difference is that you'll log in in a focused, organized, and thoughtful way.

Check your apps, emails, or other tools at the interval that makes sense for you. That might be twice a day, once a week, or randomly when you have a few spare moments. Look back at your response time plan to determine how regularly you look at notifications. Whatever your preference, be consistent about how you use notifications to streamline your workflow.

2. Exceptions to the Notification Rule

I will concede an exception to my "turn off notifications" advice. In some situations, you've got to be reachable. As a parent, the school must be able to contact you if your child is injured or ill. In business, you may make your living on the whims of the stock market. Business owners may need to be available for security system alerts or human resources crises. Similarly, medical professionals, especially those working in emergency or urgent care, must make themselves available when on call. These are just examples, you'll have to judge whether or not your digital life warrants disruption for an exception.

If you must be instantly reachable, then settle on one communication method with notifications turned on for urgent matters. If your device allows, mark the relevant business or personal contact as a VIP so their communication cuts through your do not disturb mode, if you can use that on your phone.

3. How to Check Notifications Efficiently

When it's time to check your notifications, have a process to efficiently check and act upon each notification. By doing this at set times, you'll be processing clusters of notifications in batches, a big nod to efficiency.

When dealing with notifications, you'll likely follow this four-step plan:

- Read to gather information communicated.

- Send quick replies in the moment.

- Diarize any action items arising to act on them fully when you have time.

- If possible, archive or delete anything you won't need to see again.

If your business has a high volume of emails or social notifications, consider assigning a staff member to act as gatekeeper to ensure that genuine communications don't get lost in the spam and noise. If you're working alone, dedicate time to gatekeeping on a weekly or daily basis.

Clustering your notification time improves your productivity, protects your daily task list, and keeps stress at bay. Sounds good, right? Go turn off unnecessary notifications now.

9
Dedicated Devices

To streamline your digital life, you need dedicated devices. This means that specific activities and tasks will only be done on one device.

Here's an example: Your mobile phone could be dedicated to phone calls, text messages, taking photographs, and Instagram. Meanwhile, your tablet, if you have one, could be for listening to music, watching videos, reading ebooks, and social media such as Facebook and Twitter. Next, you could use your computer for all email, writing, spreadsheets, photo editing, and file management.

When you dedicate devices to specific tasks, your thought patterns grow accustomed to the mindset needed to do the task at hand. Writing a report for work takes a different kind of effort than watching episodes of your favorite television shows.

1. Divide Your Digital Activities

How you divide your digital activities will be a matter of personal preference. Your choices will be unique to your hardware and the content you create or consume. A dedicated device strategy creates patterns that focus your efforts.

In part, the distinctions are a matter of personal preference. They are also a matter of practicality. Sitting at a desk in an ergonomic chair with a full size keyboard makes most people more efficient for longer form and complex tasks. By contrast, your tablet is very portable and can be there to entertain you during your transit commute or in the family room.

You'll adapt how you use devices to your preferences, the volume of information you create or consume and the amount of data you're dealing with. And, of course, you'll take into account the devices you have to work with. Some people use two mobile phones; one for home and the other for work, for example.

In some cases, you may decide to do the same task on more than one device and that's OK. This may be helpful if, for example, you're working on a writing assignment. If you typically use your computer, you may want to have the flexibility to add notes via your mobile phone when inspiration strikes. Other examples include social media, group chats, and photo editing. While dedicated devices help with efficiency and productivity, it's up to you to decide when more than one device helps rather than hinders your efforts.

2. Go Analog to Decide

If you're struggling to decide how to use your devices, I suggest you go analog for a few minutes. (See Sample 8.) Look on the download kit for the Dedicated Devices planner.

Each column notes a soon-to-be dedicated device. The form includes mobile phone, tablet, and computer to get you started. Use the blank columns to add your web-enabled television, game console, fitness watch, or other devices, if you have them.

Next, list all the digital tasks you do as the row headers down the left hand side. Email, ebooks, music, movies, television, podcasts, photography, writing, spreadsheets, team chats, and the names of your preferred social networks may all be on the list.

Finally, mark the box that intersects between the digital task row and the device you want to use for that task. Likely, you'll need a test period before you finalize how you'll organize your dedicated devices. The way you use the devices will change over time. Feel free to update your dedicated devices plan, as needed.

Sample 8: Dedicated Devices Planner

Make a list of your most common digital activities. Note which dedicated device you will devote to each. Remember that you can use the same device more than once.

Activity	Mobile	Tablet	Computer	Recorder	
Email			x		
Facebook		x			
Podcasts	x				
Netflix		x			
Instagram	x				
Photo edits			x		
Audio recording				x	
Calendar	x	x	x		
Shopping		x			
Music	x				
Writing			x		
Notes					

3. Sticking to the Plan

To accomplish using devices for dedicated purposes takes commitment. You've got to make a plan and then stick to it. Only with a full commitment can you confirm which device does what.

You may be tempted to go back. It's easy to revert to old habits. For many, social media apps are the hardest thing to streamline. No matter how you plan your digital devices, I keep reinstalling a Facebook tab on my browser and the app on my tablet and my mobile phone. You may have digital tasks that bleed over from once device to another. We're human.

4. Devices When You Travel

Travel is a key exception to the dedicated devices plan. If you, like me, prefer to travel light, you'll want to take as few devices as possible. Carry-on only is ideal in this era of excess baggage fees and intense security screenings. Bringing your mobile phone, tablet, laptop, and related cables and accessories is too much weight!

With a little planning, you can temporarily install the right combination of apps on your device of choice. You may not work as efficiently as usual, but it's a joy to travel with ease. In addition, both business travelers and leisure travelers do different things when away from the office or home. You may not need full functionality. Perhaps you can set aside certain digital tasks until you return from your trip.

10
Digital Calendars

In my opinion, digital calendars are one of the best inventions of the information age. The typed contents are always legible and easily edited. Lots of detail can be included such as the agenda, location, and other details. The information is portable and doesn't add a heavy item to your briefcase or book bag. Events can be easily synchronized between computer, mobile phone, and tablet. Specific appointments and entire calendars can be shared with one or more people with ease. Overlapping calendars allow the easy comparison of availability between work colleagues or family members. It's possible to automate scheduling, RSVPs, and reminders. Repeating events can be simply propagated indefinitely into the future. And they are difficult to lose and, if backed up, easily restored.

Many digital calendar options are available. You may use Google Calendar or the iOS calendar in your Apple device. Some email programs, such as Microsoft Outlook, include calendar functions. Larger offices have proprietary scheduling programs that are often built into project management software. If your life should include more than one digital calendar, they can usually be synchronized so that all your appointments are visible. Although, in terms of decluttering your data, I strongly urge you to pick a single calendar platform and consolidate all your appointments in one centralized place.

1. What to Include in Your Digital Calendar

Digital calendars offer us the opportunity to include an infinite amount of information for each appointment. However, it is possible to put in too much information. Each time you add something to your calendar, try to include only the essential details. If you subscribe to a series of plays at your local theater, note the date of the performance and, perhaps, the title of the play. If you know where the theater is, there's no need to waste time entering the address of the venue, for example.

> While I love digital calendars, sometimes it can be helpful to put pencil on paper to map out a project. The visual cues of the plan on paper can help you see patterns and problems that might not be visible in the digital view. To help you with this sort of planning, the download kit includes a year's worth of monthly calendar pages for analog notes to help you plan your time as part of an integrated digital life.

You may also waste time inputting events that don't require an appointment. Some things happen on regular intervals and are simply part of your day. If you regularly pick up your kids from school at 3:00 p.m., then you'll be in the habit of collecting them each school day. Professionally, if there's a team meeting every Tuesday morning, then you'll know where you need to be. Include only the appointments and related reminders that will help you. Don't create extra work typing up events that will happen anyway!

2. Schedule Digital Tasks and Digital Fun

Take time to schedule your digital activities. You get to decide when to use technology. In turn, this affirms when you're not going to use technology. You don't have to use it all the time. Frankly, a 24/7 digital life would be terrible for your physical and mental well-being and it can disrupt your sleep. It would be utterly boring. You've got to get out and live a little!

Remember you are in charge of your digital life. You also get to choose when you're going to be offline, away from your computer, and ignoring your smartphone. To do this, I recommend you separate your digital tasks from digital fun.

> For more advice on calendars and planning, I highly recommend the work of Mike Vardy at Productivityist Inc. The content he shares to help people be productive is so valuable and his philosophy aligns with the digital cleanse process in *Declutter Your Data*. I'm a big fan of his theme days approach, where each day of the week centers on a core activity. Dedicating Wednesdays to podcasting and Saturdays to family time, for example, might be in alignment with how you schedule digital tasks and digital fun. Learn more at productivityist.com/angela

Digital tasks are things you do for work or your own projects. These might include writing blog posts, checking social media feeds, creating illustrations, or editing copy. Digital fun includes all your leisure activities. Movie night, video games, Instagram, and other social media outlets are all fun digital activities. Of course, for a movie reviewer, watching movies is work, not play. That's OK. You get to decide how to define the activities in your digital life.

3. Put Your Digital Time in Your Calendar

Sample 9 is a staged excerpt from my calendar; I color code events in blue when they are digital tasks related to my professional life. Orange events are digital snippets from my personal calendar. My digital fun happens early mornings, evenings and weekends. From Monday to Friday, I schedule my work-related digital tasks, for the most part. What you can't see in this example is that I have the flexibility to move my digital appointments around other events. For example, if I'm a parent volunteer for a school field trip on Monday morning, I'll reschedule my blog writing time for the afternoon.

Note that the tasks are broadly defined. Digital work time might include writing the next blog post but the calendar doesn't have to include the details of what writing is happening.

Sample 9: Author's Google Writing Calendar

08:30 - 10:00 Me Social Media	07:00 - Me Social Media	07:00 - Me Social Media	07:00 - Me Social Media	07:00 - Me Social Media	08:30 - 10:00 Me Social Media
10:00 - ACA Social Medi	07:30 - ACA Social Medi	07:30 - ACA Social Medi	07:30 - ACA Social Medi	07:30 - ACA Social Medi	10:00 - ACA Social Media
9:30 - 11:00 Blog Writing		09:30 - 11:00 Blog Writing		09:00 - Send Shine Fri	
				09:30 - 11:00 Blog Writing	
13:00 - ACA Social Medi	13:00 - ACA Social Medi	13:00 - ACA Social Medi	13:00 - ACA Social Medi	13:00 - ACA Social Medi	
					18:30 - 21:00 Movie Night
19:00 - 20:00 Me Social Media	19:00 - 20:00 Me Social Media	19:00 - 20:00 Me Social Media	19:00 - 20:00 Me Social Media	19:00 - 20:00 Me Social Media	
21:00 - 22:00 Video Games	21:00 - 22:00 Video Games	21:00 - 22:00 Video Games		21:00 - 22:00 Video Games	

Time axis: 05:00, 06:00, 07:00, 08:00, 09:00, 10:00, 11:00, 12:00, 13:00, 14:00, 15:00, 16:00, 17:00, 18:00, 19:00, 20:00, 21:00, 22:00

4. Have a Ritual to Make the Most of Your Tech Time

For some, a simple ritual can help with the transition before and after digital tasks and digital fun. These transitional times can help focus your mind on the next activity and, at the end, clear your mind to focus on the next.

At the office, a pre-tech time ritual might include tidying the desk, turning on task lighting, locating a pencil and paper, and putting the phone on "do not disturb." The post-tech time ritual might include recharging the technology, if needed, a quick stretch and several sips of water.

At leisure, the specific tasks might change but the ritual notion remains the same.

11
The App Diet

An easy win in digital decluttering is something I call the App Diet. Simply by deleting apps from your mobile phone or tablet, you'll reduce the digital clutter in your life.

Using fewer apps can save you time with fewer screens or folders to browse through. You'll also free up some memory so you can take more pictures, download more music, or keep your favorite ebooks on your device. Costs savings may also be reflected in your mobile data usage as many apps use data, even when you're not using the app it works in the background.

You'll also lessen the load on your processor. This is especially helpful if you have an older device. As with all digital decluttering, your focus will improve as it will be easier to hone in on whatever you planned to do. As we discussed earlier, nobody needs the distractions.

Don't delay. Grab your phone or a tablet and take control of your "app-etite." It's a low-risk category of digital decluttering as a deleted app can always be reinstalled.

1. How to Reduce Your "App-etite"

Deleting unwanted apps takes just a few minutes. Start by swiping through all your screens and deleting anything that's unfamiliar. Check in each folder you've created, too. If you don't recognize an icon, odds are you haven't used the app recently. Next, peruse your apps again and delete any you rarely use. Travel apps are a great example. If you love to fly with WestJet, you know how handy its app is on travel days. Yet, you likely only fly a few days each year. The rest of the year you live without the app. Delete it after each trip and know you can always download it again, whenever needed.

Next, think about how you use your device. Think back to your dedicated devices plan. What apps do you really use? Be brutally honest and get rid of the ones that you no longer use to do tasks on your device. Also keep an eye out for redundant apps that have similar functionality. For example, you may have several photo editing apps. Keep only one to crop, rotate, or annotate your images. Easy!

Next, consider the functions that can be done more efficiently on a computer. Again, keep your dedicated devices plan in mind. Delete the apps that duplicate your computer tasks. Don't waste time fumbling on a touch-screen keyboard. Most people write much more efficiently on a full-size keyboard. If you have a surplus of word-processing apps, delete the excess. It's OK to keep one app per function for times when you are away from your computer.

Now, think about time-wasting apps. Do you use your mobile or tablet as a productivity tool? Then delete the games. Conversely, if your device is all about relaxation, delete the work apps.

Lastly, protect your essential apps. Be clear on what can't you live without. Depending on your priorities, that might be email, Instagram, or a meditation tool. Make a mental note that these apps aren't going anywhere (you can always get them again). If you accidentally deleted something essential, take a moment and download it again now.

That's it. You're done. Great job! Now, the real trick is to stay on this diet. Too often, we're wooed by shiny, new apps. It's easy to click "download." Resist the urge, as best you can.

2. Finding New Apps to Love

On occasion, give yourself permission to go on an app binge. Visit the App Store or Google Play and go download crazy. Try a bunch of unfamiliar apps and find some new favorites. Just remember to delete all the apps that don't meet your expectations so you're not introducing permanent digital clutter that you don't need.

12
Consolidate Your Data

Digital efficiency means you've got to consolidate your data. Consolidation is one of the main ways you can declutter your word processing documents, spreadsheets, databases, and audio-visual content. At its simplest, this strategy has you gather like with like so that all your photographs are in one place as are your project files, financial records, and personal history.

It may be a hard truth but you are not responsible for other people's data. In fact, you should leave their data alone and only worry about your own. This can be tricky if you share digital space with work colleagues or your spouse. Some data, photos for example, might be blended together. As much as you want to tidy up information that's not your own, resist. All you can do is take charge of your own digital footprint, and maybe inspire your partner to embark on a digital cleanse, too.

1. Data Needs a Home

When it comes to data storage, you've got three main options.

Your computer's hard drive is a classic place to consolidate your data. If it's all on your computer, then you can find it, in theory. However, I suggest this is the least reliable place to store your data. If your computer is damaged, stolen, or stops working for some other reason, all your information can be lost.

In some cases, often in work environments, you may store your information on a file server. Access to this shared resource lets you consolidate your data. If your computer stops working, your information will be intact. Correctly configured services include backups or mirrored copies of all files so the odds of a catastrophic failure are greatly reduced.

If you're serious about digital declutter, it's time to trash the Zip drive and the floppy disks. If you can still read your older storage devices, review the information and decide what, if anything, should be kept. Move only data you want to keep out of old storage to current. Once saved in a consolidated data store, the information's original home can disposed of with confidence. However, if the data is sensitive in any way, especially if it contains personal identity details or financial information, destroy it with a magnet and smash it to bits to protect your details.

Increasingly, tech users are turning to cloud storage such as Google Drive, Dropbox, iCloud, and other services. These allow you to store and access your files from anywhere. This is especially helpful if you're working on documents in more than one location or collaborating with a team. As changes are saved in real time, you'll always be working on the latest copy of the document with the right app or a browser interface.

While cloud storage is great, remember that many of these services are based in countries that permit surveillance in the interests of national security. Know your data is subject to potential scrutiny by the authorities. Security protocols on cloud-storage solutions are out of your control so there is some risk that your information could be hacked. Once hacked, how the information will be used is beyond your control. If the information you are storing is confidential or sensitive, cloud storage may not be the right solution for you.

2. File Names and Folder Structures

As you consolidate your data, consider your file naming conventions. Naming your files carefully can help you find them using the search function. When possible, add keywords, categories, and tags to aid your search for the data you need.

While the search function should find most anything you're looking for, I suggest using some folders to group broad categories of your information. Use broad categories such as photos, financial records, or personal writing to group your information. Don't get too specific or you'll be endlessly clicking through layers of folders looking for your information.

> Life happens. Births, deaths, marriages, and vacations all can interrupt your digital decluttering efforts. And so they should! In those moments where access to data is going to be a challenge, I suggest you have a single storage location – a holding tank, if you will – for any incoming data. When life returns to its normal busy pace, you can empty the holding tank and put each file in its rightful place.

Be vigilant about data you want to keep, especially older archival footage. Storage devices evolve and data can erode one byte at a time. This is known as bit rot.

Don't forget to back-up your data. Redundancy is your friend when disaster strikes! Don't let a hardware failure ruin all your efforts to consolidate your data.

3. Pick a Cloud

If you are able to accept the risks of cloud storage, including potential surveillance and hacking, cloud storage can be an excellent decluttering tool. You'll love that you can access your files, any time, from anywhere. All you need is an Internet connection and a web browser (or a mobile app). You can reliably work on the current version of your document no matter the hardware. Synchronized files are a joy. You'll also love that hardware failure no longer means a catastrophe. Yes, it's very sad when you shatter your phone but at least your data can be resurrected.

That said, don't take an ad hoc approach. With accounts on Dropbox, Google Drive, and iCloud, it's easy to fracture your cloud storage across several platforms. It may be necessary to have accounts on all these platforms because of the workflow preferences of the people and projects in your life.

After a few years, it gets tricky to remember where to find the files you need. Nothing kills productivity like the frustration of searching for files across multiple platforms. It's been a painful experience. Truthfully, I'm still reorganizing my files onto one cloud. When you have years of files to sift through it takes a lot of short sessions. Try not to do more than 30 minutes at a time to keep your sanity while processing the backlog.

3.1 Cloud storage options

To help you pick a cloud storage solution, the following are some of the available services and their rate packages as of this writing:

Dropbox
- 2 GB – free
- 1 TB – $99.00/year
- Unlimited – $21.99/user/month

iCloud
- 5 GB – free
- 50 GB – $0.99/month
- 200 GB – $2.99/month
- 2 TB – $9.99/month

Google
- 15 GB – free
- 100 GB – $1.99/month
- 1 TB – $9.99/month
- 10 TB – $99.99/month

All rates are in US funds. Rate packages noted were current in September 2017. Subject to change without notice.

3.2 Reasons for an extra cloud

I strongly recommend choosing a single cloud. Of course, if your client works via Dropbox and you work on Google Drive then you join your client on Dropbox. However, when the project is complete, archive a copy on your preferred cloud.

One last tip: If you keep accounts on more than one cloud storage service and have unused storage capacity, use that space as a backup location. For example, keep a backup of your family photos, one of your most treasured possessions, on two clouds, just in case.

13
Your Email Inbox Is an Eyesore

Confession time: How many emails are in your inbox? Be honest, at least with yourself.

Next, think about how many inboxes you have. Only one? Or do you have one for personal emails and another for work emails? If you have more than one job, volunteer in the community, or signed up for Hotmail once upon a time, you may have additional inboxes to contend with.

Let's say you have 289 inbox items. That may be high or low depending on who you're comparing yourself to. By comparison, let's say your spouse has only 12 items and a friend (who wishes to remain anonymous) has more than 75,000, how does your inbox tally compare?

This amount may not worry you or it might completely stress you. If the number causes worry or stress, you need to declutter your inbox. Don't let those excess messages hang around for long.

1. Too Many Emails

Email overload is a huge problem and it's hard to control. Long gone are the happy days of AOL's "you've got mail" chime. Today, once you share or publish your email address, you're at risk of too many emails. The quantity that means "too many" varies. For some, 300 incoming emails per day is the norm while others get fewer than 10. The volume of email you receive is a combination of a number of factors.

Let's start with spam. Spam emails are those unwanted messages sent to you unsolicited. Professional spammers use software to send spam to millions of email addresses per day. They often come from unfamiliar names, with odd subject lines and unconventional copy using strange grammar and word spacing. Even with an excellent spam filter, spam adds to the too many emails problem.

Then there's any email to which you've subscribed. Most often this category includes emails you wanted to receive at some point in the past. Membership updates from your gym. Alumni updates from your alma mater. Promotional offers from your favorite merchants and additional messages triggered by your loyalty cards. Signup is easy but at some point your subscriptions can feel like too much email.

> One of the interesting things about the surplus of email is that a personalized letter in the post is now a treat. In a sense, we're seeing a resurrection of snail mail. I love to send and receive cards and letters. If you feel inclined, send me a letter or postcard. I'd love to hear from you. My address is 225-255 Newport Drive, Port Moody, BC, V3H 5H1, Canada.

Next, is the tricky category of email you've been subscribed to involuntarily. Dropping your business in a contest entry bowl is a common source for this type of email. Despite laws regulating the fair use of email addresses and mandating formal opt-in records, many businesses don't understand that getting a business card is not permission to add someone to their list.

If you're sending bulk emails, be sure to familiarize yourself with the related privacy legislation. In the United States, consult the *Electronic Communications Privacy Act* (EPCA). In Canada, review the *Personal Information Protection and Electronic Documents Act* (PIPEDA) and Canada's Anti-Spam Legislation (CASL). Bottom line: Don't be a spammer.

By default, most social networking services send notifications by email. If you have Facebook, LinkedIn, YouTube, or other social media accounts, you may have noticed a surge in the number of emails you receive. There are ways to customize and limit the types of notifications that come by email yet many people just live with the default email clutter rather than turning off social media notification emails.

Another problem area for excess email, is group emails. When more than one person is copied on a message, reply all is often overused. A single message carbon copied (cc) to just five people can quickly create 30 or more emails in your inbox. It's an exponential problem when you're part of more than one family conversation, work group, or team project.

After all that email, I hope you have some legitimate emails from individuals. The people you want to correspond with are the reason you have email, right? I hope you can find them in the digital clutter. If you can't, this chapter offers several strategies to help turn your inbox from an eyesore into a jewel in your digital crown.

2. Chasing Inbox Zero

"Inbox zero" suggests that your email goal should be to deal with every email in your inbox promptly to keep the inbox empty. While a nice tidy goal, pursuing inbox zero isn't a productive use of your time. You can't spend all your time dealing with emails. Instead, I suggest you work on managing your incoming emails proactively using the methods outlined in the following sections. Zero isn't the goal; manageable is the target.

3. How to Tackle Your Inbox

To deal with the mess in your inbox, complete a combination of strategies each time you open your email program. I suggest you do the following things.

Don't open your email unless you have time to deal with email. This practice was inspired by Barbara Hemphill's book, *Taming the Paper Tiger* (Hemphill & Associates, 1990). The key takeaway from her writing is to touch each piece of paper, in this case email, only once. If you read the email, deal with it. There's no point in adding the stress created when you open an email and can't deal with it. Only open your email when you have time to deal with email!

When you have time for email, start by deleting spam. Don't pause to read anything legitimate when you're deleting spam. You're on a mission to clear the junk mail that the spam filter missed. Make sure your spam software is up to date and you've got the right filters set up.

Next, look at messages from VIPs. It's a good idea to curate a list of people who get top priority. With a filter in your email program, any message from them gets automatically filtered into the VIP inbox. Some are family (Hi, Dad!) or family related (a child's school) while others are people you collaborate with frequently: active clients, mentors, instructors, etc. Read each VIP email to absorb the information in it. Then, take action, if necessary. Here are the actions you'll repeat frequently:

- Send a quick reply.

- Schedule time to send a more in-depth reply at a later time.

- Delete any messages you won't need to see again.

- Archive only those emails you may need to reference in future.

Next, I suggest you look for anything that needs to be downloaded and start the download. Often, that could be new episodes of your favorite TV shows. Once downloads are in progress, delete the related email.

While downloads are downloading, read any remaining emails from individuals using the same actions used for VIP messages. Read. Take action. Schedule action. Archive or delete.

Finally, time permitting, read any email newsletters, social media notifications, crowdfunding updates, or whatever else is left over.

4. Schedule Time for Email

As part of your digital decluttering, deal with email during set times. Depending on the volume you receive, you might check once a week or, more typically, you'll check two or three times each day.

For example, you may email first thing in the morning over a cup of tea. You'll then check again after lunch. If you've got lots of "to read" messages left over when you're out of time during the work day, add an evening email reading session, too.

Keep in mind the response times you've established. This gives your work a healthy sense of urgency without a trace of panic.

5. Weekly Email Maintenance

You may also want to do a bit of weekly email maintenance. Here are some sample tasks you might complete during an email maintenance session:

1. Review your inbox for missed messages from VIP senders.

2. Delete any messages you no longer need.

3. Archive anything you overlooked during the week.

4. Reflect on your current email subscriptions.

5. Unsubscribe from email lists that no longer serve you.

6. Scan for email notifications from social networks.

7. Adjust your social media email notification settings, as required.

By doing some weekly maintenance, you'll continually declutter your inbox.

6. One Big Archive

Steve Dotto of Dotto Tech introduced me to the notion of a single, searchable archive. Having used email regularly since 1993, I was in the old-school habit of creating nested folders for all my archived messages. As per Steve's advice, I now use a single folder to archive any email I need to keep. In two years, I've archived just 2,934 messages. It's amazing what you don't need to keep. It's wonderfully easy when you can search that single archive, as needed.

7. Declare Email Bankruptcy

My next big step is to embrace the concept of email bankruptcy. I first learned this concept from an arts administrator who received more than a 1,000 emails each day. While on vacation, he would set a friendly but firm out-of-office auto-reply. It read something along the lines of "I'm on vacation until April 22. When I get back I'll be deleting all messages in my inbox. If you need to reach me, please resend your message on or after April 23."

> Another approach is to simply be honest, in advance, with your email correspondents. Use your email program's auto-reply feature to let people know you're taking a digital break. If needed, provide contact information for a virtual assistant or family member to reach if the message requires attention right away. Urgency could mean a party invitation or an elder's sudden illness or a crisis at the office.

I've also heard of people using January 1 as email bankruptcy day. They start the New Year with an empty inbox. Friends and colleagues learn that anything unresolved from the previous year has to be resent if it's still relevant. Often it's no longer relevant! I haven't had the courage to do a full delete but I have done a couple trial runs by deleting the majority of messages from an overrun reply all thread. So far, I haven't missed anything important.

If you decide to use email bankruptcy, be cautious. What works for you as a productivity strategy and digital decluttering tactic, may be perceived as arrogance or insensitivity on the part of your email correspondents. After they've gone to a lot of trouble to write to you, they may be unhappy to discover you've deleted their message and put the onus on them to reinitiate the correspondence. There's also a risk that you'll offend them so much they won't want to work with you in the future.

8. Banish "Reply All"

"Reply all" drives me batty. In general, email is a great communications tool. Easy to create. Quick to send. Simple to reply. But "reply all" makes me hate my inbox. I'm sure you can relate.

For example, let's say you have three projects on the go, each with six team members. If just one project manager sends an email to the team asking each person for input and every team member sends their response in "reply all" then you have five new messages. If everyone responds just once to all 5 of those messages, you have 25 more messages. Suddenly you've got 30 new messages to read. But wait, you've got three projects on the go so you now have 90 messages. Multiple reply threads means the information is now fragmented. Worse is when someone hijacks the thread to ask one person a question about something unrelated, adding still more email. Good luck catching up, if you happen to be offline when a "reply all" conversation hits your inbox.

This fire hose of messages can overflow your inbox. Even worse, it can bury genuine messages. You might waste time wading through multiple copies of the same messages looking for the one tidbit of new information. Sometimes you just archive the whole thread, unread. It's just too hard to find the new info. Sadly that means key pieces of information can be lost. This is not good for you, the project, or the team.

So why do people abuse the "reply all" button? In part, I think it's because everyone wants to be perceived as a contributing member of the team. They share their two cents' worth to demonstrate that contribution. In some cases, team members are focused on only one or two small projects. They don't get a lot of email so they don't see the same volume that "reply all" creates for people involved in many projects. I've also seen people wanting to mitigate their own risk. If they didn't acknowledge the email, it didn't happen.

A related problem may be the overuse of carbon copy (CC). Yes, you want to be inclusive, but maybe it's possible to be over-inclusive. It's something to think about.

What can you do about it? Education is the first step. If everyone needs your information then use "reply all" with my blessing. Remember that everyone needs to know the location of the meeting, but only the organizer needs to know your request for a gluten-free bun.

A better solution is to move your team into a different communication tool. Maybe a Facebook or LinkedIn group would work for your team? Or an internal instant-messaging service? Or a project-collaboration tool such as Basecamp or Asana? Please explore the options and banish "reply all." Your inbox will thank you.

9. Consolidate Your Email Addresses

If you've had to repeat the strategies in this chapter for multiple inboxes, it may be time to reconsider how many email addresses you have. In some situations, multiple emails are unavoidable. An address for personal use, another for work and, sometimes, a third for school. Quite often, I've found that email users, myself included, have multiple emails in each category.

Separate emails can be useful to protect your privacy. It's certainly best to deter erotic emails from your spouse from arriving at the office! This separation can help your productivity, too. School field trip notices shouldn't distract you from urgent work emails. This separation is also useful if you don't want to use one of your permanent email addresses for a short term-project; a civic political campaign, for example.

If you have to have multiple email addresses, consider having all incoming email sent to a single inbox. If, for example, you own a small business, both emails personalized to you and messages from customers perusing your website could go to the same inbox. I encourage you to have your email going into as few inboxes as possible, ideally just one. Or maybe one for personal emails and one for work.

Are you hanging on to any old email addresses just in case? I advocate for reducing the number of email addresses you have.

How many do you really need? Can you get by with just a Gmail address? Do you have the means to buy your own domain name? Can you note a particular email as temporary; say one issued by your university while you complete a certificate or degree? You'll use it while a student and then let it go when you graduate. The fewer email addresses and email inboxes you have, the easier it will be to keep your email data decluttered.

10. Inbox Is Not Your To-Do List

Remember that your inbox is not your to-do list. Don't leave action items in your inbox. Instead act on them or move them to your productivity tool. Your productivity tool might be a digital-task list or an analogy to-do list. Either system is fine as you build your integrated digital life. Just make sure all your action items are in once place so you'll be more productive.

11. Pick Subscriptions That Serve You

Please pick subscriptions that serve you! List-building is a big marketing trend right now. It's a great strategy for brands to connect with their ideal customers. Subscriptions lists can be great for customers, too. It's up to you if you want the latest information (and offers) from favorite brands delivered right to your inbox.

Have you ever been subscribed to an email newsletter you didn't want? As part of your digital decluttering, I'm giving you permission to unsubscribe. For the next month, think critically about each subscription email that lands in your inbox. Ask yourself the following questions:

- Do you really want it?

- Are you still interested in the topic?

- Do you read every issue?

- Can you get the information elsewhere?

- Is the frequency right for you?

- Does it include great discount codes?

- Is each email full of information?

- Do you like how they sell to you?

- Do you have time to read it?

If your answers are no, it's time to unsubscribe. Look for an unsubscribe link in the footer of the email. Don't feel badly, just do it. The list owners pay to have each name on the list. If you're not interested, save them some money. Save yourself time, too! If the subscription stays, now you know why you agreed to get it.

It took me a month or more to evaluate all my subscriptions. For every subscription you keep, you'll unsubscribe from several other lists. Your inbox will be rejuvenated!

Limit yourself to a few favorites to help keep the clutter out of your inbox. Use the Subscriptions That Matter List (See Sample 10, available on the download kit) to make note of the emails you want to continue receiving. Try to keep a balance amongst the various categories so you're getting information from a variety of sources.

Be very picky about your subscriptions. Each email that hits your inbox adds to your digital clutter. Once you've sorted through the backlog of subscriptions, be vigilant about any new ones that slip into your inbox.

12. Create Your Own Email System

To make email work for you, you've got to have a system. I invite you to use the strategies noted in this chapter as a starting point. I encourage you to adapt it to your work style. It won't take long to turn your inbox from an eyesore to eye candy.

Sample 10: Subscriptions That Matter List

Make note of the email subscriptions you want to receive. Try to balance your incoming newsletters across a variety of categories.

Business		News	
	1. WorkSafe		1. CBC
	2. Stock Market Report		2. CNN
	3.		3. BBC
Events	1. Evergreen Cultural Center	Gossip	1. *HELLO!* magazine
	2. Leading Moms		2.
	3		3.
Causes	1. Canadian Cancer Society	Fun	1. MyComics Page
	2. Heart & Stroke Foundation		2. Zentangle
	3.		3. *Star Wars* Books
Retailers	1. Lands' End	Health	1. *Mindful* magazine
	2. ThinkGeek		2. Allergen Report
	3. Amazon		3.
Education	1. Alumni Newsletter	Other	1. Long Beach Lodge Resort
	2.		2. Bullet Journal
	3		3.

Notes

14
Curate Your Photos and Videos

More than ever, you need to curate your photos. Without the constraints of film and developing costs, digital SLR and mobile phone cameras make it easy to take thousands of photos a year.

1. How Many Photos Do You Need?

Think for a moment. Who needs 40,000 photos of his or her six year old? A generation ago, when film reigned, it was unusual and expensive for a family to take more than a few hundred photos a decade. Go back two generations and you'll find a couple dozen photos, at most, for a lifetime. Three generations back and there might be one or two images of each wealthy person.

Today, we have the luxury of taking lots of photos but how many do we really need? This is a prime category for digital decluttering. To curate your photos, I recommend a two-pronged attack. Make a plan to deal with your new photos starting today and a concurrent plan to deal with your old photos.

Don't be a digital hoarder. I want you to spend time organizing your digital life but don't let it take over. For goodness' sake, don't keep everything! Delete is the easiest way to clear your digital clutter. This applies to photos and videos, email, and all kinds of data you can control.

2. Best Practices for New Photos

To declutter your data, it's easiest to start with your new photos. Starting today, do a few simple things to keep a handle on this data clutter. Regular, frequent effort will prevent a big backlog to sort through. If you follow these best practices for new images, you'll have a more meaningful collection and be better able to find the images you want for social sharing, and so on.

Start by reviewing the photos you take each day. This can be a relaxing and fun way to reflect on your day's adventures. As you review the photos, consider the following:

- Are there any duplicates or near duplicates that can be deleted?

- Are there any accidental images that can be deleted?

- If images are out of focus unintentionally, do you want to delete them?

- Do you have any pictures of people that show illegal or inappropriate content to delete?

- If you're using photo-editing software, do you want to tag the images with a location, event title, or other information?

- If you're using facial recognition software, do you want to label a new subject for future reference?

- Do you want to share any of the images immediately on social media?

- Do you want to file the images on your server or the cloud?

- Do you want to share stored images with family or work colleagues for future use?

3. Best Practices for Old Photos

If you've been taking photos for a while, you likely have a backlog of images to process. It's not unusual to have thousands of digital images. You may even have tens of thousands.

First, you have to decide if you want to organize your old photos. As far as digital decluttering goes, you could simply gather all the old photos in a folder and leave it at that.

However, you may want to organize some or all of these photos. Who knows what treasures you'll find from special events, to everyday milestones, and fond memories of loved ones who've passed away? If you decide to proceed, remember that this trip down memory lane can be emotionally charged so be kind to yourself and set a pace that lets you process your feelings as you work. You can stop at any time.

When you're ready to tackle your old photos, set aside some time to get started. Rather than drive yourself crazy looking at thousands of random photos, try to narrow your approach to a more manageable subset. You might select:

- A particular date range: a week, month, or year that makes sense to you.

- A specific event: a wedding, the birth of a child, a grand opening.

- A central person: yourself, the CEO, a grandchild, a celebrity.

- A centralized location: a specific city, your first home, a favorite park, office party venue.

- A memorable trip: a family holiday, business excursion, camping weekend, band trip.

Once you've selected a manageable batch of photos to review, apply the same best practices you use for your daily photographs. You might also add the task of flipping images. Quite often old negatives, slides, and prints are scanned backwards. You'll know this is necessary when the words appear in mirror image.

4. About Unflattering Photos

Take care before you delete a photo on the grounds that it's unflattering. A goofy pose, crazy hair, or an extreme fashion may all seem unflattering but please don't delete those moments. They are part of the subject's history and should be preserved.

Don't scrub people from the archive because they don't like the way they look in photos. Body image is a big topic beyond digital decluttering. Please don't delete someone based on perception of looks. Let your photo archive include the bulging tummies, scrawny arms, double chins, unexpected body hair, and the like. Instead, define unflattering as photos that misrepresent the person. That might mean deleting Grandma's accidental middle finger salute if Grandma doesn't cuss. (Or keeping it if Grandma has a sense of humor!)

5. Don't Forget Your Videos

The same strategies apply to curating your videos. Start today on new videos and plan time to review old videos until you are caught up. You may also want to add some video editing time as you organize your videos. It may be fun to put together clips to share with family, friends, and colleagues.

5.1 Live video

Have you embraced the trend for live video through social media? Facebook Live, Instagram Stories, YouTube Live, and other live-streaming social networks all make it possible for almost anyone to create and distribute video content. This emerging medium is terrific for sharing content that expresses more than words on a page. On camera, the presenter can employ facial expression, tone of voice, and body language to bolster his or her message. He or she can also add to the story by being on location or including others in the video.

The benefits of live video are huge; however, the amount of live video being created is adding to our digital clutter. If you decide to create these kinds of video, do all you can to make them great. This includes ensuring you've selected strong content or something to say of importance. You can also reduce the digital clutter by striving for higher production values. This might include using a tripod or gimbal stabilizer to make the image less shaky. A microphone and windscreen or pop filter will also help to improve the audio. Make the best video you can so you're not adding to the digital noise.

15
Smart Home Savvy

So-called smart home devices are becoming increasingly common and they bring a lot of convenience and economy to residents. You can have a smart fridge that builds your grocery list and a smart furnace that warms up your home while you commute at the end of the day. These and many other conveniences are an exciting development. However, they aren't without risk, especially when it comes to information.

1. Smart Home Devices

Before we talk about how to declutter your data in relation to smart home devices, let's talk about the kinds of devices that fall into this category. As you read this section, you may want to look at Sample 11 and then make notes on your own Smart Home Helpers worksheet (available on the download kit) to make an informal inventory. There's also space to include whether you're currently using a particular device, wish to add it to your home, or have considered it and said no, at least for now.

Sample 11: Smart Home Helpers

Use this worksheet to make notes on smart home devices. Note whether you currently use the item, wish to use it in the future, or have declined to install it.

	Device	In use	Wish list	Declined
Kitchen	1. smart fridge		x	
	2. nutrition scale	x		
	3.			
Living room	1. auto-adjust speakers		x	
	2. artificial intelligence assistant			x
	3.			
Bedroom	1. natural light simulator		x	
	2. self-adjusting humidifier		x	
	3.			
Bathroom	1. heated floor	x		
	2. touchless taps		x	
	3.			
Garage	1. proximity garage door opener			x
	2.			
	3.			
Utilities	1. app-controlled lock sets		x	
	2. motion-light dimmers	x		
	3.			
Notes				

In the kitchen, you might have a smart fridge that notes what groceries you have on hand, expiration dates, and supply levels. Some are capable of ordering re-stocks online for delivery. You may also have devices in your kitchen that weigh your food and do nutrition analysis. Digital recipe libraries can be found through web browsers and apps. Let's not forget portion-control plates and cups that track hydration.

In the living room, you may have a smart home entertainment set that knows what programs you want to watch. That same device might learn that you prefer the speakers at level 4 volume while your spouse prefers level 6. You may also have a smart speaker such as Amazon Echo or a virtual assistant such as iOS-based Siri to help you.

Bedroom arrangements can go high tech, too. You can install lights that help you fall asleep and wake you up gently by simulating sunset and sunrise. You may sleep on an auto-adjusting mattress that works to keep you asleep in the most comfortable conditions. Smart blankets, pillows, humidifiers, and fans add to your resting comfort.

When stepping into the bathroom, your feet may be warmed or cooled by a self-monitoring heated floor while the bathroom fan responds to odors and humidity. Self-flushing toilets, touchless taps, and motion-activated soap dispensers are all available. In addition, you may have a body analyzing scale, fitness tracker, or a toothbrush that provides feedback.

Your garage, too, can benefit from smart home devices including proximity sensors on your garage door opener, not to mention all the smart features built into your car.

Utilities, too, help throughout your home. Smart lightbulbs, furnaces that heat and cool in response to your family's activity, and energy-use tracking devices all exist. Add to that Wi-Fi-enabled and app-controlled power plugs, switches, dimmers, and lock sets. You'll never worry about leaving the coffee pot on again.

I'm certain this is just the beginning of smart home devices. Many more will be released in the near future and all of them dazzle with their technological developments. But there's some risk to your data as discussed in the next section.

2. Data Gathered, for Better or Worse

Many smart device companies are expanding their business models beyond things and exploring the increasingly valuable commodity data. That data is potentially collected anytime an appliance, toy, or other object is connected to the Internet through Wi-Fi or a smartphone's data link.

Not all data collection is nefarious. Often, it can be helpful. But the invasion of privacy occurs when data is collected, stored, analyzed, and used without the data creator's knowledge. Sometimes this is the user's fault for failing to read the fine print; other times it's a misunderstanding of how the device works.

Location tracking is of concern as many would like to keep their location secret. Similarly, many of these devices are designed to listen for voice commands. Jeff John Roberts noted in *Fortune* magazine, "Almost any Internet-connected device — not just phones and computers — can collect data. It's one thing to know that Google is tracking your queries, but quite another to know that mundane personal possessions may be surveilling you too." (*Fortune*, June 1, 2017). Can users trust that conversation is not recorded and kept confidential? Given the data breaches that have occurred such trust is misplaced.

In addition, it's important to understand that data privacy is governed by a wide range of moral codes. These codes vary regionally, internationally, legally, even colloquially, and international enforcement isn't always possible. This is an issue that stretches well beyond digital decluttering but it's worth mentioning as you cultivate your digital savvy.

When it comes to digital decluttering, the simplest thing is to decline smart devices in your home. No tech means no data. However, the convenience of certain devices may be worth the potential intrusion. It's up to you to decide whether to welcome a smart speaker, body analyzer, or other smart home gadget into your residence.

16
Figure out Your Privacy

No matter what sort of data we're keeping, information security and privacy are of concern. As we evaluate our digital footprint, it can be disconcerting to realize all the places where our private information can be found. In some cases, we can guard our privacy with earlier strategies in the digital decluttering process — saying no to loyalty programs, unsubscribing from email newsletters, consolidating our data, and reducing the number of places our information can be compromised.

With other types of data, especially those where we have control over the content being shared, such as social media, we can make decisions about how much information to share.

1. The 3Ps

As a framework, I've developed a self-assessment process I call the 3Ps. It's my solution to one of the most common social media objections. People worry about sharing too much online and the resulting loss of privacy. I understand the concern.

If you're using social media in your private life, nothing obligates you to share on a social network. What stays offline, stays private. It's your choice to share (or not) with family and friends or to interact with others who share your hobby. What you share is your choice. However, if you are using social networks for business purposes, you're going to have to share something. In the 3P framework you divide yourself into three parts: professional, personal, and private.

1.1 Professional

Your professional part is fully public. You share expertise, experience, anecdotes, details about your job, and information about any products or services your company offers. Sharing about your professional life can help your brand with sales and marketing. It can also position you for your next job or entrepreneurial venture. What you share publicly helps establish credibility, cultivate a network, and demonstrate authority.

1.2 Personal

To be successful online in business, you also need to share another part of yourself that I call the personal part, the next third of your 3P. Your personal part might include a love of hockey, a passion for rescue dogs, and a commitment to creative journaling. This is the part that humanizes you. It makes you a complete person not just a selling machine. It allows you to establish rapport and garner trust.

You share to find mutual interests as a lead into in-depth conversations. Your willingness to share more than just sales messages and marketing banter makes you a whole person. This is really important. Who you are and how you relate to people has to be more than shop talk. You can't be all about business all the time.

Through your online posts, comments, and interactions you must blend your professional part with your personal part. Remember this is social networking, and even if it's conducted digitally, you are still interacting with real people. The personal things you share can make it more enjoyable to do business together.

1.3 Private

The private part of yourself stays offline. You decide to keep details of your hemorrhoids, money troubles, and off-color humor private. Politics and religion are often kept private, too, just like a dinner party with the extended family. If you're not sure what to keep private, ask yourself two questions: What do you want to hide from your Mom? What would embarrass you if it appeared on the front page of a newspaper? The answers to those two questions make up your private life. If you want to keep it private, keep it offline. You choose. If you don't share it, it's not online. You are in control. (Well, almost in control. Remember that others can quote your contentious comments and share photos or videos of other embarrassing moments. That's a big topic for another day.)

1.4 Divide and blend

How to express the divide and the blend between the professional, personal, and private parts of your life is entirely up to you. Every person's answer will be unique. To help you think through what's public, personal, or private in your life, see Sample 12, and use the Privacy Self-Assessment worksheet on the download kit.

Sample 12: Privacy Self-Assessment

List elements that you self-define as professional, personal, or private.

Professional	Personal	Private
writer, author of four books	married, parent	suffered with postpartum depression
professional public speaker	lives in surburban Vancouver	
instructor, teacher, believes in lifelong learning	loves *Star Wars*, beaches, doodling	was an informal caregiver to elderly relative with Alzheimer's
expertise in learning design, content planning, digital decluttering, online communities		

As you can see in the example, which is about me, by the way, you begin to see the lines that divide. Note that I have now made private parts into personal parts in the interests of illustrating the 3P.

Another element of this is to navigate how to manage our personal brand in relation to our company's brand whether we are the business owner or an employee. The two have to be in balance — distinct from one another — yet, they must be in harmony or authenticity is frayed.

2. Be Authentic

Expressing authenticity can be difficult. It requires a deep sense of self-awareness; an understanding of our true values and expression. It also requires the ability to resist the norm; to adopt cultural and social convention as desired without artificially adding layers of society's expectations to fit a prescribed image. In other words, authenticity is about you, not others.

Share only what you're comfortable sharing. Don't create an artificial self online. I'd rather you shared a minimal amount and were true to yourself. Faking it will not get you anywhere online or in life. Authenticity is the nobler path. It's also the path to less digital clutter.

In *Reader's Digest*, Olympian and mental health advocate Clara Hughes commented on her decision to share a photo on social media showing herself sad and serious. She noted, "Sometimes being real with others also helps you be more real with yourself."(*Reader's Digest*, May 2017). As in Clara's experience, we can all benefit from some more balanced representations of our true feelings and experiences. Authenticity comes, in part, from not having to spend so much time curating content to create the perception of a perfect life.

If you're accustomed to sharing a polished version of yourself through social media and other digital interactions, it can be difficult to switch to a truer, less filtered expression of yourself. Rather than make the leap all at once, start with small adjustments. Being authentic can start with sharing honest reactions to a moving film or sharing a recipe that suits your dietary restrictions. Incrementally, as you get more comfortable, increase the authenticity quotient until you are expressing yourself genuinely.

Authenticity supports digital trust. Your data trail tells your story. As R "Ray" Wang wrote in *Disrupting Digital Business*, "People and organizations must earn trust through their actions across their relationships. Trust can be expanded to gain influence, create engagement, and foster relationships. Trust can also be lost if you lack credibility, or if you show dishonesty or other bad behaviors." The more authentically you share, the more you'll be able to build trust — a hot commodity in this digital age.

17
Connect with People

In a digital life, we can connect with more people than ever before. Gone are the divides of geography, politics, ethnicity, and economics. Social sharing makes it easier to find people who share your interests and search makes it easier to jointly research those interests. As Chris Brogan said in an email, "It's easier to connect with people and for people to connect with you if they understand that you're on similar paths. If they understand what you are doing, what you offer, where you're going, they'll know whether or not they want to communicate with you." Connecting with people is a choice. As you declutter your data, think carefully about the people with whom you connect. Some will contribute meaningfully to your data; others will not.

1. Focus on True Friends

The people you connect with online will contribute a lot to your digital footprint. You will create content to share with them and they, in turn, will create content for you to consume. That content might be original thoughts in text, family photos, or videos from a memorable event. Content takes many forms and it travels in many ways: through email, social media, shared calendars, and more.

The challenge comes when the volume of friends we engage with grows to be a big group. The more friends you have, the more people there are to talk to and listen to. That large number can become unwieldy quickly and it's easy to be overrun with data.

As you make decisions about digital friendships, keep in mind that the human brain can only maintain about 150 relationships at a time. That includes everyone from your family members and friends from university to your work colleagues plus your medical team, schoolteachers, and the clerk at the grocery checkout. Luckily, technology allows us to increase the number of relationships we can maintain by aiding memory and providing context to help us recall each person.

However, even with technology to help you, I encourage you to be cautious when it comes to how many digital friendships you accept. It helps to stick to your preset criteria, rather than accepting every friend request. Your criteria might mean people you know in person, people who share your interests, people who support the same causes, people in your family, or any other conditions you choose to select.

> Sometimes online friendships can be awkward. You may feel obligated to accept a friend request on Facebook but you don't really want to interact with that person. Luckily, Facebook provides an unfollow option that prevents the person's information from appearing in your news feed without unfriending him or her. You'll still be able to check his or her page, if you want a quick update.

Friendships ebb and flow over time. Older friendships may be treasured, forever connections. Others may be connections that have run their course as your location, interests, or other factors change. It's OK to sever the connection, which is another great way to declutter your data.

2. Don't Forget Your Fans

If you do work that involves contact with customers, clients, donors, or other supporters, you may have a digital relationship with them. Even workers who are in the public eye, such as members of the local government, have to consider parameters for digital relationships.

As with friends, your fans are going to consume your content and, in some cases, share content with you. If information or marketing materials are part of your business plan, you're going to want as many people seeing your information as possible. I encourage you to think about your criteria for how much digital clutter you can tolerate from this group. Product inquiries, bookings, service requests, and social chitchat are great. Bullying behavior, racist remarks, sexism, homophobia, and others are not.

Depending on the scope of your work, your fan base may include thousands of people in multiple locations. How you choose to handle the data that comes from this group will be a business decision that best serves what you can do.

The lines between friends and fans can get blurry sometimes. Your hairstylist might evolve from service provider to friend, for example. It's up to you to decide which category fits.

3. Pick Your Experts

As the world gets increasingly connected and the volume of information grows exponentially every year, it can be exhausting to sift through the information available on a given subject. To combat this element of information overload, I highly recommend you pick your experts. These will be your go-to resources for information who you trust to share reliable information and expertise. Let your experts do the research on current events, best practices, and new tools for each subject of interest.

Your list of experts will be unique to your interests and professional obligations. Use the Trusted Experts List (see Sample 13; it's also on the download kit) to start recording your go-to sources.

Each person's expert list will be different and that's okay. While your spouse might be interested in cooking and football, your child might be interested in video games and Taekwondo. Interests can change over time. Our go-to experts can change, too. Think of it as a fluid list of helpers you control to meet your needs.

As we're talking about digital living in this book, as an example, I'll share a list of my trusted experts. I've included mostly digital living experts who can help you on your journey to declutter your data. Please note that some experts are individuals while others are groups publishing content under a company name.

Sample 13: Trusted Experts List

List your trusted experts here.

Expert	Comments
Social Media Camp	cultural impacts of social media
Social Media Examiner	social media marketing
Rebecca Coleman	social media education
Sean Smith, The Digital Hallway	social media parenting
Vicki McLeod, #Untrending	mindful social media
Ian Cleary, Razor Social	content marketing
Tara Hunt, Truly Social	content strategy
Steve Dotto, Dotto Tech	technology solutions
Viveka von Rosen	LinkedIn expert
Mike Vardy, Productivityist	digital productivity
Dorien Morin-van Dam, More in Media	mediasocial video

Notes

Research an audio editor to help with podcasts.

4. Give up on Toxic People

Toxic people hide in plain sight. Online and in person, they'll undermine your confidence, ruin your concentration, and detract from your life's work. Toxic people can also make you cry, raise your blood pressure, and cultivate frustration. Don't let toxic people surround you.

As a framework for dealing with toxic people online, I like the model some schoolchildren are taught. They use WITS (www.witsprogram.ca) to deal with peer conflict. This simple four-step program develops conflict resolution skills around a common vocabulary:

1. Walk away

2. Ignore

3. Talk it out

4. Seek help

Adults can follow that same advice when dealing with toxic people online. It may seem simplistic but sometimes the simple solutions are best. Losing the toxicity reduces your digital clutter, too.

To walk away in a virtual environment, you can unfriend and unfollow. Depending on the level of toxicity, Facebook provides several options. You can unfollow, make a friend an acquaintance, curate a "toxic friends" list, unfriend, or even block a toxic person. Similarly, on Twitter and other tools you can use lists, unfollow, or block. Look for similar options on whatever platforms you use.

If you have to sift through hundreds or thousands of names, unfriending and unfollowing can be a time-consuming activity. To make the task more manageable, you could unfriend/unfollow next time you see that toxic person in your feed. Or, you could set aside some blocks of time to systematically work through your lists from A-Z. If you do this, work in small batches. In addition, there are tools such as ManageFlitter that allow you to set criteria to unfollow a bulk batch of Twitter accounts. For example, you might unfollow any account with the generic egg profile photo, or any account that's been inactive for a year or more.

Ignoring a toxic person online takes a certain amount of discipline on your part. When he or she turns up in your newsfeed, skim past whatever he or she has to say. Not always easy to do but worthwhile if you're better off without the toxic person.

It's possible you have to interact with the toxic person. You could try the "talk it out" strategy. An in-person conversation would be ideal so that you can read body language and hear tone. If a face-to-face meeting isn't practical, a phone call is the next best alternative. Your last resort should be written feedback. Too often, sensitive issues can be misconstrued in writing and you end up aggravating the problem rather than resolving it. Also, remember that the toxic person may not realize his or her actions are offensive or negative. Proceed as diplomatically as you can.

Finally, if all else fails, you have the option to seek help. Most social networks have the functionality to report abusive users. Twitter Support offers a helpful how-to, as does Facebook Help Center. You may also be able to reach out to an administrator for assistance.

I hope you have zero toxic people in your life. If you are dealing with them, know you are not alone! It's a frustrating, maddening thing to experience but you can take steps to give up on toxic people.

18
Social Networks and Online Communities

How many social networks do you belong to? In 2017, Smart Insights shared statistics on social media use worldwide. The findings note that 2.789 billion people globally are active social media users. That's 37 percent of all the people on the planet! (www.smartinsights.com/social-media-marketing/social-media-strategy/new-global-social-media-research/, accessed September, 2017). Do you consider yourself to be an active social media user? I do! Before I started my digital cleanse I had about 450 accounts. Many of these accounts were created for research purposes and it was time to close them. If you're doing a digital cleanse, I suspect you have some excess social media log-ins, too.

To get a better sense of your social media use, take a few minutes to refer back to your Digital Footprint Inventory. Look more deeply at the social networks and online communities on the sheet and record more detail on the Social Media Snapshot (Sample 14; available on the download kit).

Sample 14: Social Media Snapshot

Review your social media accounts and inventory them here.

Account	Notes
Facebook profile	my personal profile
Facebook group	Social Media Mindfully group
Facebook group	women entrepreneurs group
Facebook group	writers' group for sharing ideas
Facebook page	for Angela Crocker & Associates
Facebook page	for *Declutter Your Data* book
Twitter	my personal profile, used publicly
Instagram	my personal profile, used publicly
Hashtag	#digitalcleanse
Hashtag	#digitalmamma
Hashtag	#declutteryourdata
LindkedIn	my personal profile, business use
YouTube	video channel
Pinterest	account unused in many years
Snapchat	account rarely used since set-up

Comments:

Consider deleting accounts on Pinterest and Snapchat.

Check old files for abandoned social media accounts.

1. Take Charge of Social Media

A digital cleanse is a good time to revisit your social networks including any custom online communities you belong to. Think about each account and ask yourself the following questions:

- Do I use this social network all the time?

- Do my friends/colleagues use this network?

- Do I use this social network at home?

- Do I use this social network for work?

- Do I create content suitable to share on this network?

- Do I know how to use this account?

- Is this account for a current project?

- Does this account amuse me when I'm bored?

- Does the network still exist?

If you answered no to any of those questions, it might be time to break up with one or more social networks.

Before you delete, deactivate, or close your account, consider whether or not it's important to you (or your business) to keep control of your name. I'm aware of 21 others named Angela Crocker who use social media. Maybe you have doppelgangers, too? Also, consider that you may need to keep select accounts as the log-in for other purposes. For example, don't delete your Facebook profile if you manage any Facebook pages or groups.

When you're 100 percent ready to break up with a social network, proceed with the delete, deactivate, or close procedure for that network. Generally, you'll find the appropriate link on your profile page or on the help center page. It will be tricky to find. The social networks don't want you to leave the party. It's OK if you're ready to go.

In some cases, there is a waiting period before your account is fully closed. Those social networks give you an out in case you change your mind. A mistake is possible at any time. And there's extra risk if your digital cleanse ritual includes a nice glass of wine!

2. Forget about Social Media

As you declutter your data, another approach to social media is to forget about it. If you don't open an account, it can't create any digital clutter.

As I wrote this book, I was surprised by how many people don't use social media at all. Often for professional reasons, they don't want to risk doing something perceived as inappropriate on social media. In other cases, their employer mandates that they have no social media accounts. Still others make the choice to forego social media to free up time to spend on other pursuits or to step away from the negative impacts on their self-esteem.

Remember that using social media and joining online communities is a choice. If you decide to say no, it's an easy part of your data decluttering.

3. Social Media Invitation Etiquette

If you are a member of a social network, you may have noticed that there are evolving etiquette standards. In particular, invitations to events and groups are a huge source of digital clutter. Unfortunately, once you have a connection to another person, he or she can invite you to events, add you to groups, request that you follow something, or send other invitations.

The challenge is that many people don't stop and think before issuing an invitation. They assume you'll be interested or, more likely, don't want to take the time to carefully filter who they invite. This is especially true with invitations to events that happen in other cities. Yes, you'd travel to attend a wedding but you're not going to fly across the country to go to a lunch and learn session. I'll leave it up to you to decide if unwelcome invitations are issued innocently or are a result of laziness.

This type of digital clutter is hard to manage but there are some things you can do. Make a commitment to respond to each invitation as it arrives. A quick click on no, decline, or not interested removes the event from your digital clutter. If you RSVP yes or maybe, then you're interested enough to tolerate the related digital clutter. In the event you are added to a group without prior notice, assess the group when you first see it. If it seems of interest, stay. If not, leave the group immediately.

At the same time, think carefully about your own use of invitations. Please don't create events, groups, or chats unnecessarily. If you do, include only the people you know are interested. They'll welcome the information. If you're not sure, invest some time getting to know them better before you extend an invite.

4. Delete Unused Groups

As you declutter your data, you may discover you have groups, events, chats, or other social media commodities that are unused. Anything that's dormant and not needed for archival purposes should be deleted. Sometimes we hang on to things for too long. Give yourself permission to push delete or pass on the admin role to someone who wants to take the lead.

19
Take a Digital Vacation

Somewhere along the last few years, we lost the weekend, that hard-fought break from overwork created just a century ago. While technology has spread to make our lives easier, it has also given us unprecedented connectivity. We can be reached at all hours on any day unless we take action to set up boundaries to shield ourselves from the influx of data. As Steve Dotto said in his March 2017 webinar, "Dealing with Distraction," "train yourself to be less available."

With endless data arriving by phone, email, and social media, we don't have the time to process all the incoming information fully. Even if we've successfully decluttered our data, there's still information coming in each day. Claire Suddath noted in the article "So Hard to Say Goodbye," *Bloomberg Businessweek* (November 4-10, 2013 edition), "checking e-mail in the bathroom and sleeping with your cell phone by your bed are now considered normal." We don't have to accept that that's OK. More importantly, we have to acknowledge what prevents us from connecting with our bodies, our family, and our community. As I've said before, it's important to find the right balance to achieve an integrated digital life.

You don't have to make a big deal about going offline. Just step away. To some extent this takes the pressure off if you decide you want to break your fast to do something. A digital vacation is for your benefit alone and you get to decide how to do it.

1. Value of Doing Nothing

In our hyperconnected, post-industrial world, the value in doing nothing at all has been lost. Yet, there is value in stillness. Silence gifts us the opportunity to consider other points of view, to contemplate, to check in with ourselves, to just be. Yet, at every opportunity — on the bus, in the waiting room, by the playground — we check and recheck our phones.

Part of the problem is that technology has become a boredom buster. Continuous entertainment is available if we want to access it. As Sherry Turkle wrote in her book *Alone Together* (Basic Books, 2017), "There's less tolerance for the boring bits in life." Technology is buffering that tolerance with regular access to boredom relief.

#Untrending is both the title and the theme of Vicki McLeod's book in which she discusses the importance of using social media mindfully. In addition to being a social media aficionado (check out her Instagram Stories!), Vicki advocates getting offline. She writes, "Getting offline creates perspective. It reminds us that we are flesh and blood. That our hearts beat in this body, that our feet touch this ground, and our limbs swing out with ease (or creakily)." For more visit www.vickimcleod.com/angela.

Another aspect of the problem is society's push to see us being constantly productive. A person at rest is lazy, not relaxed. In public especially, we want to garner good opinion. Those on a digital cleanse know that time offline is recharging, not lazy.

Furthermore, your "doing nothing" may include technology and that's OK. With the right discipline you can use technology as needed. Maybe you want to binge watch something on Netflix, level up on a video game, or dance to your favorite playlist. Just as a walk on the beach or time with your watercolors can be recharging for some, digital can be recharging for others. As you adapt your digital life, you get to choose.

2. Get over FOMO and Embrace JOMO

The fear of missing out (FOMO) grips many digital citizens. Are you afraid of what you'll miss if you're not online? If you find yourself checking email in real time, compelled to read every status update on Facebook, and constantly checking Instagram to stay abreast of the latest, you've got a problem. The compulsion to stay online disconnects you from the people, passions, and projects that fuel your soul. Rather than worry about what you're missing online, I encourage you to embrace the joy of missing out (JOMO).

The joy of missing out might mean spending time with family. A morning of LEGO with a happy child or a tea date with a beloved grandmother who has no interest in digital anything can give you alternate perspectives.

While offline, you might talk about flowers, clothes, world events, or family history. Each conversation can be joyful in its own way and potentially rich in information you won't find online. Perfect moments come when we can simply sit and hold a loved one's hand. Just be. Think about who you want to spend time with.

> For a more academic look at JOMO, I highly recommend *The Joy of Missing Out: Finding Balance in a Wired World* (New Society Publishers, 2015). In her book, Christina Crook writes, "By understanding our online habits, we can form new ones – as we seek to be fully human in a smartphone world."

The joy of missing out also means doing more of the things you love. Writing in a journal, cycling, swimming, and beachcombing are all offline activities. Doodle with fine art supplies or browse bookstores. Think about what you love to do. To help you figure out what gives you joy, complete the JOMO journaling pages available on the download kit. See Sample 15.

While you may document lots of your activities with photos, try leaving the camera alone. It's very freeing to just enjoy the moment. No need to freeze frame your kids in action to take a photo. Nor do you need to recreate those perfect moments. Just commit them to memory. My dear friend, Moira Bridgman, gave me an amazing

Sample 15: Digital Vacation Journal

Date: September 9

Without your phone, tablet, or computer what would you do for a day? List some analog projects you'd like to work on.

walk by the river

go through my grandmother's china and decide what to keep

color some pages in my adult coloring books

call my aunt overseas to chat

Date: September 9

During your digital vacation what will you think about?

plans for my next home renovation

multigenerational activities for the next family reunion

how to read as many books as possible, poolside

Sample 15: Continued

Take notes during your digital vacation. Who do you spend your time with? What do you do? How do you feel?	
Sunday	travel day, feeling tired
Monday	museum, pool time, keep checking for phone
Tuesday	beach day, wondering what's happening back home
Wednesday	shopping, excursion, enjoyed haggling
Thursday	guided excursion, took lots of photos, feels good to be in the moment
Friday	travel day, happy to be going home
Saturday	unpacking, laundry, delaying return to digital life

piece of advice for my wedding day. She told me, "You won't remember what you saw but you will remember how you felt." I've lived that truth as much as possible and I hope you will, too.

While undertaking a digital cleanse, I encourage you to plan time away from your technology. Spend time with the people you love. Do the things you enjoy.

3. Tech-Free Time

Figuring out how to incorporate tech-free time in your life can start small. While there are offline retreats, unplugged vacations, and other extended experiences available, most people start on a less grandiose scale. You don't have to go to extremes to reap the benefits of some unplugged time.

Look at your daily schedule to see where you can set aside your technology and ignore your data for a little while. Maybe you enjoy the sunrise early each morning or, perhaps, create an evening ritual before bed. Other alternatives include a specific meal time, your fitness workout, or the hour after your kids get home from school. Having family rules about no technology at the dinner table and no phones in the bedrooms overnight are other good options. As Baratunde Thurston noted in *Fast Company*'s August 2014 edition in the article "Unplugging's a Beach," "A digital detox can be as reinvigorating as an island getaway, but routine, short tech breaks can be even more refreshing." Don't we all need refreshing?

Another option is to set aside technology for a full day each week. This may align with your spiritual practice. Removing digital from your day of contemplation becomes a welcome part of the ritual. A full day each week frees you from your data for longer periods of time.

If you decide to go offline, inform key family members and business colleagues in advance. You don't want them to worry when you're unreachable. If you have set times you go offline daily or weekly, they will get to know those rhythms and be unconcerned if there's a delay in your replies.

As you gain confidence and comfort with tech free time, you may decide to disconnect during a vacation. Since 2013, *Condé-Nast Traveler*, *Bloomberg Businessweek*, *Travel & Leisure*, Fast Company, and other leading magazines have published stories about digital vacations, digital detox retreats, and other unplugged adventures. Traveling overseas often creates an unplugged vacation when roaming data charges are prohibitive. Or, maybe, you'll escape to a rural or wilderness area that has no Internet or cellular service. Developing countries also have much different Internet access, often the speeds are less than North Americans are accustomed to. A staycation in your own home can be unplugged, if you want it to be.

Even if you travel somewhere where you could get online, challenge yourself to skip the GPS and embrace the experience when you get lost. Immerse yourself in the local language and attempt to communicate without a translator app or digital phrasebook. Try and figure out how something works without consulting a search engine.

Interestingly, *Allure* magazine reported in its January 2017 edition that, "57% of millennials intend to do a digital detox on their next vacation." That's a lot of unplugged adventurers and I'm excited for all they will experience.

4. Sabbatical versus Convenience

A conversation with Paul Holmes, cofounder of Social Media Camp, got me thinking about the notion of digital convenience. While there are many benefits to tech-free time and there's adventure in trying to cope without instant access to information, sometimes our unplugged sessions need a little flexibility.

While you are working on decluttering your data and see the value of an integrated digital life that includes both online and offline time, you don't have to be a slave to hard and fast rules.

Some types of technology can be helpful to maintain a healthy relationship: An ongoing text chat with your best friend, WhatsApp messages to a grieving friend, or video chats with a loved one are all good examples. These reinforce one-on-one relationships with people who can't always be in the same room at the same time. The key is to make these check-ins brief and efficient so you don't get sucked in.

Set rules for yourself to define your digital detox. Unplug except for text messaging a select group of VIPs. Or continue taking digital photos with your mobile phone but plan to share after your offline time. The choice is yours.

5. Go Analog

There is friction between the analog and digital worlds. Individuals have to smooth the edges in ways that work for them. You may choose to declutter some of your data by taking it offline.

As much as I love digital calendars, I acknowledge that there's a trend returning many to paper agenda books. Handwritten journals, to-do lists, whiteboard explorations, and more are increasingly frequent. In part, I think this is a response to our need to spend less time on devices.

There's also an aesthetic element for many people. The visual appeal of a bullet journal or sticker-filled planner is an enjoyable part of the process. And that's OK. Anyone who's played with crayons can recall the immersive, tactile experience of hands-on creativity that keeps us in the moment.

20
Pursue Your Passions with Abandon

My advice to pursue your passions is another, deeper layer of your digital cleanse. Too much of our digital lives is stuck in what our jobs require or things we feel obligated to do online. I want to encourage you to pursue your passions at every opportunity. If it's something you love, then you'll always have energy for it.

Do you know what your passions are? Passions can take many forms. Here are some ideas to get you started:

- Soap making
- Spring skiing
- Tiny homes
- Disneyland
- Breastfeeding
- Choral music
- *Star Wars*

Some of these are brands with loyal followings. Others, I would call social movements. Still others are just for fun. What thrills you? What fuels your curiosity? What energizes and rejuvenates you? Whatever your answer, you'll have found your passions.

Ideally your passions become your vocation but we're not all so lucky! Instead, fuel your soul with the things you love. You'll be amazed at how much energy you find to devote to them.

21
Fighting Fake News

Fake news is everywhere and it spreads like wildfire across the Internet. Some days it can be exhausting trying to figure out what is the truth, from a certain point of view. In the digital clutter context, fake news is a trap door filled with unwanted data.

1. Vetting Information

I suggest the solution to fake news lies, in part, in learning to vet information sources. Reliable sources are vital to the success of your digital cleanse. Instead, know that it can be helpful to pick some reliable sources of information. Choose some that present opposing points of view so you are informed about the issues in a balanced way. There are a number of factors to consider when assessing the reliability of a source.

2. Technical Considerations

Before you even click on the news item, examine the URL. If the web address includes excessive sub-domains or odd extensions, it's a less reliable source. If the link looks legitimate, check the publication date. Content lives on the web for years, so old information can easily be recirculated. Make sure what you're reading is current. Also, review the contact page. If it includes a legitimate location, phone number, email address, and contact form, it's more likely to be a reputable source.

Also, consider the links on the page itself. Does the article include a reasonable number of links? Consider whether they are helpful or click bait. Also, look closely at any pop-ups, if you're being bombarded with requests to sign up or other offers, the site may be less reputable. Finally, check to see if you were clearly informed of cookie tracking, those little bits of code that tell web hosts your computer has visited their site. It's common practice to use them and best practice to inform visitors that they are being tracked.

3. Content Creator

Next, consider the source. Content from a media outlet adds to the content's credibility. Think about the differences in reputations for longstanding news outlets. Network news is different than cable news just as commercial radio and public broadcasting are different. Not better or worse, just different. On the web, your potential sources stretch far beyond traditional news outlets. However, you can apply a similar filter when you assess an online magazine or blog.

In addition to the outlet, look at the content creator's biography. Try to find out the author's background. Is he or she a recognized journalist, published writer, academic, or other authority on the subject? Maybe, like parent bloggers and foodies, he or she is living with the information every day and has expertise to share.

4. Consider Bias

As you look at sources and content creators, be alert to bias. Bias suggests prejudice in favor of a particular point of view. There's politics in the opposing views of every subject from military spending to breastfeeding. Both new and longstanding media outlets and content creators may have agendas that influence their content. Find multiple sources for the same information. If the story is reported in a balanced way in more than one reputable place, your confidence in the information should rise.

Don't forget to read more than the headline. An attention-grabbing title might suck you in, which is fine if it's backed up by a solid article with detail. Attention-grabbing headlines that lead to nowhere of substance are called click bait. Fake news outlets use click bait a lot.

5. Follow the Money

Nothing is created without some sort of funding. Advertising might be your first clue about the validity of the source. If the page has more ads than content, be suspicious.

Look again at the content creator. The money says something different if the author on payroll is a reputable journalist than when he or she is a lobbyist for a special interest group. Similarly, check to see if opinions are being swayed by corporate sponsorship. Not all sponsorships involve undue influence, but some do.

6. Research Ethics

As you read, look for evidence of solid research to support the article. Seek articles that reference primary research from a thought leader, academic, or subject matter expert. If data is quoted from a survey or poll, look to see if it was conducted by a reputable polling company such as Gallup or Ipsos or conducted under the authority of an accredited university.

Secondary research should also be included. This may appear as links to multiple sources of information. It may also include quotes from previously published content, interviews, or other media on the topic.

You can also check the validity of the information. If the news seems too good to be true or sensational in any way, odds are it's fake news. Scope out the topic on Snopes.com or other fact checking websites.

7. Funny Pages

When assessing fake news, it's important to apply satire savvy. Outlandish stories could be a deliberate attempt to make us laugh or to highlight a problem through absurdity. Satire websites such as

TheOnion.com, TheBeaverton.com, and CBC's This is That clearly note that they are poking fun at a topic.

8. Emotional Triggers

Strong emotional responses can also be a hint that you are reading fake news. If you find yourself unduly angry or devastatingly upset, get in touch with your emotions. Affirm if the content is the source of your emotional response. Often stories that make you angry or cry are exaggerated beyond the truth to manipulate your emotions.

9. Savvy Friends

Figuring out fake news can be hard and exhausting. If you haven't got the time or energy to vet your sources, identify a trusted friend who does. That news-savvy friend can save you some time if you're confident in his or her fake news filter.

Being alert to fake news and seeking reputable sources can reduce your information overload. As a bonus, it reduces the digital clutter in your life, too.

22
Capturing Ideas

Good news! At any moment, you may be inspired with a bright idea or simply remember a task that needs doing. Unfortunately, our short-term memories don't hold onto those ideas for long. To avoid distracting yourself trying to remember, put all your ideas in one place. The goal is to document the idea, inspiration, or task so you don't forget. By writing it down, you improve focus on your current task.

1. An Effective Productivity Approach

Capturing your ideas when you have them is not a new productivity strategy. I've heard variations discussed by many students and writers. By following three simple steps, you increase your productivity.

First, capture any idea as it occurs to you. Jot it down quickly and continue with your current task. Capture personal and professional ALL in one place. Once the idea is documented, forget about it until step two.

Next, schedule 30-60 minutes every day to review your idea notes. During this time, take immediate action on any item that can be completed during this daily appointment for one.

Finally, schedule time to execute more complex tasks. Make an appointment with yourself to pay your bills, get a haircut, or review the proofs of your new book. Simply moving the idea to your calendar means you're done with that item for today.

This approach echoes what we've already talked about in the chapters called Turn off Notifications and Your Email Inbox Is an Eyesore. To simplify the digital cleanse, I've purposely repeated simple processes rather than having a different dance routine for each action.

2. Ways to Capture Your Ideas

As with other steps in the digital decluttering process, how to capture your ideas is a matter of personal preference. Some people prefer a digital solution while others go analog with pen and paper.

There are a wide range of digital solutions. Evernote, Google Drive, Basecamp, and many other applications. A spreadsheet or word processing document works, too. Please use what works for you and your workflow.

Analog solutions are varied, too. You can use a scrap of paper, looseleaf paper, or a notebook. I must admit to a deep love of pretty and geeky notebooks so I've always got a few spares in my desk drawer. I use pencils and I've seen friends use the full rainbow of colored pens.

Ideas can be fleeting. We get distracted and it's easy to lose our train of thought. Ideally, you'll pop the idea straight into your inspiration file. If that doesn't work in your current circumstances, you can do the following:

- Call yourself and leave a voicemail.
- Email yourself the gist of the idea.
- Snag a photograph with your smartphone.
- Grab a screenshot with your tablet.
- Send your spouse a text.
- Keep a notebook and pencil in your nightstand to jot it down.
- Write it in the dust on your dashboard.

I've done all of these, as circumstances warranted. Don't feel silly. Use the tools you have on hand before the inspiration leaves you forever. An image or a few keywords are all you need to re-trigger the inspiration when you can transfer it to your inspiration file.

Remember that you are going to be inspired by the ideas in your file. You're not going to use them verbatim. I'm not advocating for copyright infringement or intellectual property theft. However, you should feel free to use your inspiration as a springboard for your own ideas.

Your inspiration file will grow and evolve over many years. What inspired you in 2006 may be of no interest in 2018. You'll use some ideas and not others. That's OK. It's much easier to create something inspiring from a catalyst in your notes. Use your inspiration file as a starting point.

3. Digitize Your Analog Notes

You can be a bit sneaky in your execution of this method. Use pencil in a notebook to capture ideas and then digitize them by scanning or photographing the page. You can even use a specially formatted notebook that will turn your handwriting into searchable text. Your quick scribbles and sketches can easily be converted to digital notes, when needed.

23
Digital Parenting

Children of all ages are exposed to technology every day. Whether they use computers or see their parents using smartphones, devices and data are everywhere. If you have children in your life, their data is part of your digital clutter. Train them how to deal with digital clutter early in life and it won't be a headache for them (or you) to sort later.

Although teachers are tasked with instructing students about technology, online communities, Internet research, and more, they are often ill-equipped to fulfill this requirement. Some schools embrace online communities and devices while others ban them outright. In some cases, the teacher is unfamiliar with the technology. In others, the teacher uses the technology but has reservations about ever-evolving best practices. Most often, teachers need to get on with the business of teaching the curriculum. Technology can enhance a topic but it can also distract from the lesson.

Given teachers' variable roles in teaching children how to live an integrated digital life, it falls to parents and guardians to step in. Yet, parents are also floundering with the issues, concerns, and tactics. The goal is to teach kids how to use technology, manage their data, and be productive digital citizens. How to do that and at what age to start is a hotly debated topic. In my opinion, you can never start too young.

To get a sense of your perspective on kids and technology, ponder the question, how would you entertain a child without technology? Record your answer on the Parenting Priorities worksheet on the download kit (see Sample 16).

Sample 16: Parenting Priorities

Date: October 27
How would you entertain a child without technology?
Build a fort with blankets and furniture
Go for a walk in nature
Make music with household objects
Play rhyming word games
Nap
Read a book together
Cook stone soup with whatever is in the fridge
Play classic games such as Go Fish and Checkers
Plant a garden

1. Model Best Practices

Children and teens learn from what they see so one of the best things parents can do is model best practices. All of the digital decluttering strategies in this book are potential lessons. It's important to talk to your children about response times, email management, social media etiquette, and the online/offline blend or balance. We also have to teach them about some of the darker sides such as dealing with toxic people and spam.

The most important thing is to keep an open dialogue with children and teens about why you're teaching them these strategies and how it will make their digital lives better. Of course, you'll have to adapt your comments to the age of the child: A preschooler will learn about mean people while a teen will learn about cyberbullying.

It's also important not to stereotype kids based on their gender, age, ability, or other factors. You cannot assume they will intuitively know what to do. Instead, assume they need guidance to figure out their digital footprint. Prepare them to be digital citizens.

2. Cyber Dangers Are Real

Much has been written about the perils for kids online. Their emerging sense of self, limited critical thinking skills, and susceptibility to peer pressure add to their vulnerability.

There are real online dangers for kids, just as there are real dangers for kids traveling through your neighborhood. Just as you teach them to be bear aware, alert to traffic, and stranger danger, you must also teach them about cyberbullying, phishing, luring, and explicit content. The specifics of those lessons are beyond the scope of this book but it's key to know that each can add to your family's digital clutter. The more trouble your kids get into online, the more data you've got to unravel.

> For more help guiding young people through the dangers and opportunities of digital life, turn to Sean Smith of The Digital Hallway. His program is designed to teach parents, teachers, and teens about the good and bad aspects of social media. Visit thedigitalhallway.ca/angela.

3. Kids' Digital Clutter

Like adults, children and teens have digital clutter. Most of it will be on their mobile phones and tablets with some extra on any computers they use.

It's important to be knowledgeable about what devices your kids are using. If they have spending money, a family sanctioned mobile phone may not be their only device. Knowing what they have will help you find their digital clutter.

Prime information to look for includes your kids' passwords; both the password that unlocks their device and the passwords for any accounts they have created. As kids get older, you'll have to begin to trust them with this information. How old depends on the kid and your parenting style. One parent might grant all access to a ten-year-old. Another may make their kid wait until age 14 to have unfettered access to devices. In general, I recommend waiting as long as possible.

Kids' digital clutter looks much the same as yours including photos, videos, social media, email, and so on. Help them learn to manage it by discussing strategies such as how to deal with new photos at the end of each day. Make them alert to the perils of live video; walking through the house on video chat may just expose a naked parent stepping out of the shower.

Gaming is another area where children and teens have a lot of digital clutter. They often try out numerous games and jump on the bandwagon for the latest craze. Even with parental controls and purchase authorization controls in place, kids are clever and they can often figure out a workaround. The cost of these games is also an issue, especially with freemium games that start out free but offer in-app purchases. Discovering, preventing, tracking, and reversing charges on your credit card adds to your digital clutter.

To get your kids involved in the *Declutter Your Data* process, have them fill in selected worksheets from the download kit included with this book.

4. Posted with Permission

Empower your kids to speak up for best digital behavior. Remind them to speak out when a friend takes an unwanted photo, while sleeping at slumber party, for example. They can be vocal and deny the friend permission to post that image. Parents, too, may need to ask permission to post, especially as tweens and teens gain a sense of themselves in the wider world.

Parents, too, should think carefully before they post. There is a fine line between sharing parenting experiences and exploiting your kid's life stories. Be alert to the kind of content you are posting about your child and think about what it says about him or her in the future. Shaming or other negative behaviors are not okay. Celebrating milestones and family events are OK. Remember, you too, should feel confident that the content you're sharing is posted with permission.

Another form of permission may come from parent to child. Letting them know when it's appropriate to use technology, what kinds of sharing are suitable in the moment, and use of shared storage solutions. For example, sharing publicly about a family vacation may put the family home in danger of being robbed or vandalized. You have to teach your family to use caution to ensure your possessions will all be there upon your return.

5. Location Tracking

Location services are a point of tension for parents. Some parents use them to track their kids' location and find it a comfort to know where they are as the child walks home from school. Others go further using Big Brother to track a child's every move at the mall, in the park, and elsewhere. Those location services allow others to track where your child is, too. While stalking is rare, it does happen, especially if your children and teens are participating in online communities.

By contrast, there's something to be said for raising resilient, independent kids who don't rely on technology and data to navigate the world. When they lose their device, it's an important life lesson about taking care of their things.

6. School Rules

School policies about technology and Internet access vary widely. Some have a strict "no devices" policy and some may supply devices while others require students to bring tablets or laptops. Some allow students to use their mobile data on campus while others confiscate devices. The school rules that apply to your children impact their digital footprint.

Whether students bring their own devices or use school provided computers, odds are they use these for some schoolwork. School issued email and shared workspaces in Office365, Google Classroom, or other collaborative tools are the norm. More digital clutter, I'm afraid.

Communication with the school office can add to your digital clutter, too, with notices from the administrators, teachers, sports teams, school clubs, and the parent advisory council. In my experience, these missives are often redundant but you have to read them all to find the new information applicable to your child.

7. Family Internet Rules

To help manage your family's digital life, I recommend documenting your family Internet rules. Start with simple language that toddlers and preschoolers will understand and let the rules evolve over time as your kids get older.

Many of the rules will echo aspects of the digital cleanse process while others reinforce digital life lessons. The following are some examples:

- Never share your last name.
- Never share where you live.
- Always tell a parent if someone asks where you live.
- Never tell if you're going on vacation.
- Always tell a parent if someone asks if you are going on vacation.
- Never tell how old you are.
- Never use bad words.
- Never talk about private parts.
- No photos of private parts.
- Always tell a parent if someone asks about your private parts.
- It's OK to share photos but never send photos of where we are.
- Ask a parent before joining a new conversation.
- A parent may review chat history at any time to make sure it's kid appropriate.
- The following chat apps are approved _____
- The following game apps are approved _____
- The following social media apps are approved _____
- Always use good manners. Be kind.

- Treat people with respect. Remember you are speaking to a person not a machine.

- Turn off geotagging. Don't reveal your location in your data.

- Headphone volume must be low. Take care of your hearing.

- We agree that ending tech time requires a heads up including a time specific countdown.

- Screen time is limited to _____ per session.

- On school days, technology is turned off from 8:00 p.m. to 7:00 a.m.

- Treat technology gently. Devices are fragile.

- Clean your screens regularly.

- No technology at the dining table.

- No technology in the bathroom.

You'll also want to talk about the consequences for breaking the rules. Loss of screen time, device grounding, extra chores, and more could be consequences of meaning in your family. Remember, the consequences can apply to parents as well as kids.

If you think it would be helpful in your family, turn the rules list into a contract with each member of the family signing the bottom to show their understanding and agreement. (See Sample 17.)

Sample 17: Family Internet Rules

List your family's Internet rules. Note consequences for breaking the rules. Add signatures at the bottom to make this a contract.

Date: March 8	
Name and age of child(ren): Jack (10) Jill (12)	
Rule 1	Never share personal information such as your age or location.
Rule 2	Always tell a parent if someone online asks for personal information.
Rule 3	Roblox is the only approved game app.
Rule 4	Always use good manners. Remember you are talking with real people.
Rule 5	Screen time is limited to 30 minutes per session.
Rule 6	All technology is turned off between 8:00 p.m. and 7:00 a.m.
Rule 7	No technology in the bathroom, bedroom, or dining room.
Consequences	If a rule is broken, the consequence is no screens for one day. If a rule is broken again, the consequences doubles to two days. If the rule is broken three or more times, the device may be taken away for a month.
Signatures	Jack Jill Mom Dad

24
Digital Estate Planning

Nobody wants to talk about death. Our own mortality is an uncomfortable subject. However, the responsible thing to do is to get our affairs in order before we die. This will benefit and comfort our loved ones after our passing during an inevitably difficult time.

While I am not a lawyer, I have been the executrix of two estates in recent years. Dealing with funerals, probate, possessions, and bequests had me reexamine my own estate planning in more detail.

Ideally, we all have a power of attorney in place that a trustee can act on our behalf if we are incapacitated. In addition, a last will and testament is recommended to ensure that your affairs are dealt with after death.

What's missing from these legal documents is information on the scope of your digital footprint and your wishes for your digital legacy. At one extreme, you may want to delete all record of your existence; something that's hard to do given the multiple facets of a digital life. At the other extreme, you may want to have your digital life preserved as a record of your contributions.

In addition to your own affairs, you may need to ensure elders in your family have their affairs in order. This includes their digital affairs so that you can help them access their email, financial, and other data.

While it may not yet be part of legal estate planning, this chapter is designed to help you prepare so that your executor or family member can take charge of your digital life when you die.

1. Estate Practicalities

On a practical level, you've got to think about your personal digital footprint and the future of your online business. Make arrangements in advance to reduce the stress for your executor and protect your heirs, especially if they are minors.

As an individual, you'll have numerous accounts from social media to email and more. Giving your executor access to your passwords is a tricky business. For security, you won't want to reveal these while you're living but the methods to pass them on are limited. Although not very secure, you could leave a spreadsheet listing your log-ins and passwords. Other solutions include services that manage your passwords for you. Services such as 1Password (1password.com), Dashlane (www.dashlane.com), or LastPass (www.lastpass.com) help you log in and all you have to remember is one key password. By leaving your executor the key, he or she can access your digital footprint when the time comes. LastPass even lets you designate an emergency access contact.

With some social networks you can plan in advance for your passing. With others, your family members or executor will have to deal with them. Here's what to do with some of the biggest social networks:

- Facebook allows you to designate a legacy contact in your security settings. This person will be able to access your profile to manage your content and post a memorial message.

- Google, including YouTube and Gmail, allows you to set up an inactive account manager who is automatically contacted after an extended period of inactivity.

- Instagram allows your executor or family member to request your account be memorialized upon death. Once complete, the account will be static with no new content or followers.

- LinkedIn allows your executor or family member to request removal of a deceased person's profile.

- Twitter allows your executor or family member to report the death and delete the account.

- Other accounts on your Digital Footprint Inventory will need investigation.

Beyond social media, you'll have a variety of other digital accounts to be dealt with from your loyalty program cards to your financial accounts. Digital business assets must also be inventoried including affiliate marketing obligations, domain registry succession planning, and more. Business-wise, there may be even more critical pieces to protect if you hold patents, copyright, or other intellectual property.

As we move forward, I anticipate lawyers will be able to draft a digital representation agreement, akin to the representation agreement for advanced health-care directives. This document would help further protect your digital assets and make your wishes known.

2. Wishes for Digital Assets

When you have time, think about your wishes for the bequest of your digital assets. You're the best one to decide whether accounts should be deleted or memorialized. You may want to instruct your executor to delete any not safe/suitable for work (NSFW) emails or files, for example. Famously, author Terry Pratchett asked that the hard drive containing his unfinished writing be run over by a steam roller so that any last unpolished glimpses of *DiscWorld* would be erased.

Think also about the digital possessions you own. This might include an extensive library of music and movies on iTunes or Google Play Store. It may also include virtual tickets for one or more upcoming events. Digital debt may also come into play if you've supported a crowdfunding project or have tuition to pay.

It's also a good idea to think about what you want your digital footprint to tell future generations. If you know your great, great grandchildren will read your social media posts and emails, what version of the truth do you want them to read? Genuine life experience includes the good, the bad, and the ugly.

If you've created lots of online content, and especially if it's generating income, you may need to appoint a manager to look after your digital legacy. Consider whether your executor is up to the task. Any income streams from digital sales, affiliate income, and the like would go to your heirs, administered by your executor. Having a clear plan in place is especially important for passive streams of income.

Whatever your desires, talk with your executor, make notes to pass on, and consult your lawyer to formalize those elements that can be noted under the law.

25
Think Like a Librarian

Your digital cleanse is, in large part, about organizing your digital clutter. It's time for you to think like a librarian. Neil Gaiman is quoted as saying, "Google can bring you back 10,000 answers, a librarian can bring you back to the right one." (www.neilgaiman. com, accessed September, 2017) You are the best librarian for your unique digital footprint and all its contents.

As you sort through your data, consider how you will use that information in the future. Things that will be accessed again are treated differently from things used in several contexts. Consider adding details such as keywords, tags and categories for an effective search at a later date. It's time to curate your data so you can find what you're looking for. Cultivate the librarian mindset.

1. Need to Know, Nice to Know

The amount of effort you put into organizing a piece of information may depend whether it's something you need to know or something that's nice to know.

Things that you need to know are essential. You won't be able to get by without these details. This might include passwords and contact information or it could include the essays for your current course or a report for your boss. Need to know information gets extra attention to ensure it's accessible.

Nice to know items are extras. They enhance other information but aren't vital and losing them isn't the end of the world. Details for a party held three years ago aren't vital. Nor is the soccer team's old game roster. Less attention is required and if you misplace the file, it won't be a disaster.

As you consider your data, you get to decide which information needs more or less attention. Your definition of what's necessary and what's nice is the standard.

2. Fake News and Click Bait

As we talked about in an earlier chapter, fake news is rampant and you've got to filter for it. In your own files, look for potential fake news pitfalls. You may have some research notes that are copied from an uncredited source. Or maybe, in a fit of anger, you wrote a long, derogatory speech about someone.

As you find these fake news archives, clearly flag the issues or delete them.

Part III

Maintaining Your Decluttered State

Once you've decluttered your data, your attention will shift to maintenance mode. Keeping a happy balance between the digital and analog components of your life requires some ongoing effort. Data is an ever-changing element of your life. In this part, you'll learn about ways to maintain your decluttered state and make a lifelong commitment to digital happiness.

26
The Art of Digital Living

You've come a long way on your digital decluttering journey. Ideally, you've come to better balance between online and offline activities and between digital and analog strategies. It should feel good!

Remember that digital decluttering is an ongoing process. You have to be vigilant. Think of it like a weight-loss maintenance program.

Remember that digital living requires you to take charge of your digital footprint. How you store passwords, manage your email, and gather your photos all contribute (or detract) from the quality of your digital life.

Take a moment to reflect on your experience with *Declutter Your Data*. How did you do? What will you do again? See Sample 18 and then use the Reflections on Digital Decluttering journaling page on the download kit to capture your thoughts.

Sample 18: Reflections on Digital Decluttering

Date: September 1

Reflect on the *Declutter Your Data* process. How did you do? What will you do again?

Some parts of digital decluttering were fast for me. I was able to quickly implement the app diet, digital calendar, fake news strategies, and more.

I struggle to declutter my photos. I have so many photos! I may just archive all my old photos or maybe I'll sort them over time.

I definitely have a better understanding of where to find my information. It's much easier to navigate my hard drive now.

I'll have to stay on top of my email every week. My inbox grows so quickly!

I'm rethinking social media. I might limit myself to just one or two accounts.

I'm practicing saying no to stop digital clutter before it becomes part of my life.

1. Digital Decluttering Maintenance

Before we wrap up, take a few minutes to think about maintenance. A little bit of regular maintenance will prevent you from having to declutter in a big way again and again. There are many different ways you can continue to look after your data.

1.1 Ongoing check-ins

One of the easiest ways to maintain your digital cleanse, is to check-in with your data regularly. Set a schedule that works for you. It could be a part of your end-of-day activities. It could be a weekly tidying task or a monthly maintenance memo. Or maybe it works best for you to simply add this as an annual part of spring cleaning. How you choose to maintain your data depends on your workflow and the volume of data you're creating. A maintenance schedule of any sort will help keep you organized.

1.2 Revisit troubleshooting tactics

If you notice your data blooming in a particular area, take action to deal with the problem sooner than later. Relapses are common especially with high-volume areas such as loyalty programs, email, and photographs. Digital estate planning and digital parenting can also be hot spots as circumstances change. If you don't remember what to do, revisit the relevant chapter in this book for guidance.

1.3 Hide in plain sight

To truly take control of your data and have technology work for you, you've got to be able to see at a glance what's available to you.

If you've applied the advice in *Declutter Your Data* you have a single email archive, only the apps you need, an organized photo library, and one cloud to store it all on. The last step is to make sure it's all visible. Don't bury your access points in folders within folders. Make them as close to top level as possible. Similarly, unpack your apps so you can see them on your desktop, home screen, or dock.

Your technology should be equally accessible. Don't tuck it all away in a drawer or box. Have it out where you can get at it. What are you using on a regular basis? Think about your dedicated devices and how you use them. I embrace the idea of giving each item a specific home. If you're not using your tablet, place it on your nightstand. That way you'll always know where to find it.

2. Quest for Digital Happiness

In a lot of ways, *Declutter your Data* is about the quest for digital happiness. It's about finding that personalized balance between digital and analog. It's also about coming to terms with the digital assets and technologies that improve life without overwhelming it. That blend is very personal and often we are wooed by the promise of digital nirvana when we peek at what others are doing online.

Here's one last big piece of advice: Let your quest for digital happiness be a personal journey.

Integrate digital into your life as suits you. Be mindful of how and when you use technology. Understand your privacy and take steps to guard it. Let GPS guide you unless you feel like getting lost. The blend that's right for you is unique and it will change over time.

Take charge of your data. Use it to enhance relationships but be aware it can also hurt them. Use it to document your life but also enjoy life's experiences. Be clear on what you want to say and what you don't. Once you know what you want to say, tell it well. Write, record, photograph to the best of your ability. Tell a story. Share with gusto. Make it memorable. Turn it into a shared experience.

2.1 Beyond the basics

Digital happiness can't happen without basic comforts: clean water, food to eat, somewhere to sleep, a sense of safety, good health, community, and a sense of belonging. Digital can provide some escape to the challenges when these things aren't in place but it's a bandage, a soother, not happiness.

The decision to seek digital happiness has to be voluntary. In fact, it's a privilege. Some will be satisfied as they are, even if that means digital chaos. And that's OK.

Others will be dissatisfied in some way but unsure how.

Still others rail against the notion of digital altogether. Sure, they might use technology because they have to for work but they're not happy about adding tech to their leisure time.

Others, including the readers of this book, are looking to take action to make changes in their data and technology use. Whether they know it or not they are mapping their journey to increased digital happiness.

2.2 Define your own happiness

Take responsibility for your own digital happiness. This is your quest. You may share the journey with family, friends, or colleagues but ultimately only you can define your own happiness. Think about what drove you to deal with your digital clutter. Your reasons can help you define happiness.

Digital happiness might be the opportunity to consume content — movies, magazines, music. You may also include the opportunity to create content — film, record, write. Or maybe the gadgetry, both tools and toys, bring little bits of joy into your life. There's something wonderfully cheery about the tune an LG dishwasher plays when the cycle is complete. Let's not forget seat warmers in the car on a wintry night and the delights of Internet radio bringing the world within earshot.

Digital happiness also includes your tribe — big or small — the people you connect with personally, professionally, socially. The delineations are blurring. That's why I talk about living an integrated life.

Generosity makes you happy. Be generous. Be quick to like, comment, encourage, and engage. Be liberal in sharing your knowledge. Be present in all you do. Be mindful of digital distraction in all parts of your life.

2.3 Be mindful

We need to understand mindfulness and how it fits in our digital lives. We'll be happier with the right tools: apps and technology. We'll be happier interacting with stories and truth and authenticity. No need to hide behind a web of lies. Be truthful. Be authentic. Be clear on your boundaries. Think about privacy. Again. Consider the following questions:

- How does technology make you feel?

- What are your limits?

- When do you need a tech break?

- Conversely, when do you need a tech fix?

- What are your points of frustration?

- What do you need to learn?

- What is digital clutter to you?

The quest for digital happiness is an exploration of answers to all of these questions and more.

Think mindfully about how technology fits into your lifestyle. Adapt your commute to include or exclude technology. Use technology when you travel or not at all. Seek print books or ebooks as suits your preference. Add music or silence as the soundtrack of your life. Consider whether you want to live in a smart home, or not.

Be alert to the links between technology and emotion. Don't let fake news run away with your common sense.

Take imperfect action. Good enough can still make you happy.

Whatever sort of data you have, cluttered or decluttered, edit it to bring you closer to success in your quest for digital happiness.

2.4 Going forward

Declutter Your Data has provided strategies for dealing with a wide range of digital clutter. I'd love to hear your successes and challenges throughout the *Declutter Your Data* process. If I've missed something you're struggling with, please drop me a note and I'll gladly help you find additional resources.

I'm @AngelaCrocker on Twitter and Instagram. You'll also find me on Facebook and LinkedIn. Find links to my social media accounts at AngelaCrocker.com plus my email and snail mail addresses. And don't forget you can ask questions through my website. There's a special web page for *Declutter Your Data* readers at AngelaCrocker.com/DYD.

Wherever your digital journey takes you, I trust I've been a helpful guide. Whether your data is a source of information or entertainment, I hope you've calmed the chaos as much as you need to proceed without stress and frustration. Keep the quest for digital happiness top of mind and you'll find your way.

Download Kit

Please enter the URL you see in the box below into a web browser on your computer to access and use the download kit.

www.self-counsel.com/updates/declutter/18kit.htm

The following files are included on the download kit:

- Bonus chapter on digital physical fitness
- Worksheets so you can follow along in decluttering as you read the book
- Resources for further reading
- — And more!